African Herdboy

by the same author

LITTLE BOAT BOY
THE THIRTEENTH STONE
PETER HOLT, P.K.
THE STORY OF INDIA
THE WISHING APPLE TREE
THE RED BARN CLUB
SEARCH FOR A GOLDEN BIRD
RING OF FATE
THE PROMISE OF THE ROSE
THE MISSING VIOLIN
THE SILVER MANGO TREE
THE EMERALD CLUE
THE RED SCARF
WHITE FAWN OF PHALERA
ROMANY GIRL
DANCING PRINCESS
RIDE, ZARINA, RIDE
MYSTERY AT THE HOUSE-OF-THE-FISH
DEFIANT BRIDE

African Herdboy
A Story of the Masai

◘◘◘◘◘

Jean Bothwell

Illustrated by Carl Owens

Harcourt Brace Jovanovich, Inc.
New York

**CENTRAL MISSOURI
STATE UNIVERSITY**
Warrensburg,
Missouri

Text copyright © 1970 by Jean Bothwell
Illustrations copyright © 1970 by Harcourt Brace Jovanovich, Inc.

All rights reserved. No part of this publication may be reproduced or transmitted in any form or by any means, electronic or mechanical, including photocopy, recording, or any information storage and retrieval system, without permission in writing from the publisher.

FIRST EDITION
ISBN 0-15-201630-9
Library of Congress Catalog Card Number: 76-117615

PRINTED IN THE UNITED STATES OF AMERICA

FOR Rosalys H. Hall—
*as courageous as Batian
and an enduring friend*

Contents

AUTHOR'S NOTE 9

1 A Masai Tribe Goes Walking 15
2 Siamanta Builds a House 25
3 The Airplane 41
4 Visit to the Armorers 49
5 Boma Meeting 64
6 Sky Ride 73
7 Looking Backward and Looking Forward 87
8 A Gift for Batian 95
9 The Whistling Thorn 102
10 A Gourd Full of Cow Fat 113

Author's Note

The Masai of East Africa are an ancient people. It is thought they came from the Nile River country, long years ago. Their language is not like that of any other African tribe, but it is similar to the speech of some present-day people who live on the Nile. And the most pronounced physical characteristics of the Masai —fine features, lithe, copper-tinted bodies—all point to Nilo-Hamitic beginnings.

Along the way from long ago to modern times, from Egypt to Kenya and Tanzania in East Africa, they have intermarried with some of the tribes met in passing, so that their features have changed here and there. Yet the Masai are still the most distinctive people in their region.

They are nomadic, moving about to seek water and pasturage for their herds of cattle and flocks of sheep and goats. This has brought them into head-on collision with the conservationists who want to protect the wild animals of East Africa from possible complete extinction. But the Masai claim that in the beginning Engai (God) gave to them only, as his favorite people, the right of cattle ownership, so that the needs of domestic cattle should come first as opposed to those of the different species of beasts that roam East Africa's lovely plains.

The Masai are not cultivators of the lands they claim to be theirs alone. This is partly because they never stay long enough in a place for a crop to mature. The rest of the reason is their way of life. Only the women eat vegetable food, though they enjoy ceremonial meats. The men live commonly on milk and blood, both obtainable from their herds. Within the tribe a man's place, his wealth and standing, is reckoned by the number of animals he owns, though he is reluctant to speak the number aloud. He considers his cattle as part of his family and cares for them as if they were his children.

There are two types of dwellings used among the Masai. One is the separate family hut of one room. A group of these are enclosed by a thornbush-and-sapling-pole fence, in the center of which the cattle of all the tribe are kept at night for protection from wild animals. The word *boma* means literally the thorn fence, but has come to mean the village unit as well, "those living within the fence." The other dwelling is the *manyatta,* which may be divided into several rooms. It is the place where the young men, sometimes from several villages, go to live after they have qualified as warriors, at about the age of fifteen. They begin to possess and build up their own herds of cattle after that time, but the manyatta, though of the same construction as the boma hut, has no fence, so the warriors look after their animals themselves.

The Masai do not have a king or prince or any other type of hereditary chieftain. Nowadays the government helps them choose a leader, one of their own Elders, who is go-between to the government on all tribal matters. The *Laibon* (hereditary medicine men) hand down their knowledge of healing herbs and the power to predict the future from father to son. They and the current chief Elder are greatly respected by all the tribe.

Then there is the District Officer, usually a European, who is responsible to the government at Nairobi, the capital of Kenya, or Mombasa, the capital of Tanzania, for all that goes on among the Masai tribes scattered about. They address him as *Bwana,* which is a Swahili word understood by all the Masai as meaning "master."

In spite of the many changes that have come to these ancient wanderers in recent years, they maintain their ancestral pride of a birth different from all others. That pride shows in a man's walk and in his dealings, when he has to have any, with all other Africans, as well as with Europeans and Americans. His superior bearing is easily sensed everywhere. It is the more notable as he has few material possessions to support such pride, and his clothing is distinctly primitive.

The force of modern times is bringing change to these people, and they are resisting it. There are not as many of them as there used to be. Except in cases where some have been willing to accept government help in the form of veterinary aid for their cattle, the herds look scrawny and neglected. The old pride and other scruples prevent some owners from accepting sprays and injections for their animals.

In recent years a few are realizing that in order to fight for possession of their lands against the encroachments of agriculture and the rivalry of wild animals' needs, they must let some of their children be educated, if only to help in the legal battles that they see coming. There are already a number of educated Masai men in the government councils at Nairobi and Mombasa.

This is the story of Batian, a young herdboy, named for an ancient Masai chief, and the crisis of decision he brought to his tribe because of a brave act —the defense of a beloved pet from a raiding lion.

JEAN BOTHWELL

Autumn, 1969

CHARACTERS

Batian, a young herdboy of the Masai tribe of East Africa
Ole Kantai, his father
Siamanta, his mother
Nalo, his older sister
Soko and *Guhano,* herdboy friends
Tipis, fifteen, his cousin
Ole Likimani, most senior Elder
The Laibon, medicine man
The Ol Kunoni, an inferior tribe of Masai who are blacksmiths and metalworkers
Martin Bolling, an Englishman, the District Officer, called Bwana
Nyenpe, Batian's heifer calf

1

A Masai Tribe Goes Walking

The great herd of cattle was unusually quiet, plodding along patiently in the dust their own hoofs stirred up. There were sheep and goats among them, and they were the vocal ones. The sheep baaed continuously. The goats were even noisier, protesting such activity on a warm day. They were hungry and wanted to stop and browse on the bushes they passed, but the watchful men and boys prodded them on.

Batian was glad that his herding was not as difficult as usual today. He was only one of many who walked on all sides of the cattle and sheep and goats to keep them together on their march to the new home the tribe was seeking. The long spears of the moranes (warriors) were protection, too, from the possible sudden leap of a daring lion.

It was October, "the last month of hunger," and rain was not far off, but it was still hot and dry, and neither

man nor animal was comfortable. It was no time for any tribe of people to be moving about in East Africa. These of the Masai tribe—men, women, and children—had had no choice that morning except to start out, taking all their animals and their few possessions with them.

Batian shifted the two-day-old calf he carried onto his other hip and wiped a hot hand on the drape of faded red cloth that covered his body to below the knees. Even the handle of his small spear was slippery with sweat.

He would not be allowed to use a real morane-sized spear until he was big enough to carry it, fifteen years old for most boys. But owning even a small spear now meant that some day he would be a man and could carry one of the great seven-foot weapons. Women and girls did not carry spears, he thought with satisfaction. Would a great spear with its sharp tip be more than the weight of the little calf? He wondered about that, idly,

then fell to thinking about the circumstances of the morning that had started the tribe in search of another home.

At dawn everything had begun as usual. The day was peaceful and even pleasant in spite of the warmth and drying waterholes and scant pasture. If nothing had happened, they could have stayed in that place until the rain came again.

The women leisurely prepared their own and the children's food after all of them had joined in the daily dry-weather prayer to Engai (God), which they faithfully performed as soon as the pastures began to wither.

When the morning meal was over, the women and the elder children had spread out among the cattle waiting within the boma (the thorn fence) to be led out to pasture. Before the gates were opened, the beasts must be made more comfortable for their day under the blue African sky. All the ticks that searching fingers could find must be pulled off. Such care of their animals was understood by every child. The family wealth was in cattle, as many as could be acquired, though the exact number that each man possessed was never mentioned. That would be boasting and tempting trouble in one form or another.

Batian had a good idea of how many his father owned, for he had counted them. It was easy to do. Each family had its private mark on its animals. But he would never tell that they were more than a hundred, increased every year when the calves came. The number didn't stay the same from year to year, of course. Once in a while a cow died, and there was the occasional ox used at a time of ceremonial and feasting.

Later that morning the tended cattle had been taken to pasture by all the village herdboys, and the little calf that Batian now carried had been left on a comfortable bed inside his family's hut. It would be safe there from any danger.

As he and the other boys followed the cattle out onto the plain, they had seen a group of women carrying baskets, starting for a session of barter with a neighboring tribe that was not Masai. They would bring back the vegetables and grain that the women and children of the boma ate. His mother was not among them . . . no one went every day. The Masai did not make gardens. They were rarely in a place long enough to raise a crop such as cereal grain. And even if they did linger in a chosen place, it was not their custom to plant anything.

The happening that occurred afterward, toward noon, when the bartering women had returned, was the cause of the present march.

An old, old man had died.

The whole boma knew he was ill. He had lain quietly on his bullock-skin pallet for weeks, and though it was felt but not expressed that he would never get up again and walk about, not even his family had expected him to die that morning.

It had happened quickly when the time came—so quickly that they hadn't had a chance to remove all his ornaments to give to the relatives before the weak spark of life flickered out. Others would have liked having his buffalo-horn armbands, his ear pieces, and his necklaces if they could have been removed beforehand. As it was, these treasured possessions had to be left on the body.

Worst of all was the other calamity, always dreaded among the Masai when death was near. The family hadn't had time to lift the old man on his pallet and carry him out of the boma to die.

The entire village was annoyed with that family. Now all of them would have to pack up and move, burning their huts before going, because the whole boma, not one hut alone, was polluted by that death within its circling fence. No one could stay in that village any longer because the spirit of the tired old man might hover there.

It would have been the same if someone young had died in the boma, or a cow, or a prized ox during the time when all the cattle were within the enclosure for the night. The tribe believed in abundant life, but they tried to ignore death. They never again spoke the dead person's name, and they did not bury the body. The fine earth of the Masai country would be poisoned if any body lay in it, and grass would never grow again on that spot.

It was a bad time of year to move. That was the chief reason for the village anger. Batian had listened to the grownups' grumblings after the call had come to the herdboys to bring in all the cattle and prepare to march. Since they had some pasturage and water there, the angriest said, they could have stayed another month through the dry season until the rain. It was a good place they had found after their last march. No one wanted to leave it.

A Masai Tribe Goes Walking

There was still another reason for the anger of a few families. It was almost time for the observance of their sons' coming of age. Five boys were to be circumcised in preparation. All the boma would take part in the feasting when the boys received their spears and shields.

How much delay this forced march would cause, Batian could not tell. It rested with Ole Likimani, their chief Elder. The Masai never decided anything quickly. It was their custom to talk and talk and talk first. His family had a special interest in the occasion this year. Though he hadn't an older brother, there was his cousin Tipis, whose father did not have many animals and couldn't afford to give even one to the armorers who were making the new equipment for all the boys. So Ole Kantai, Batian's father, would have to pay for everything for Tipis. Sheep or goats perhaps for the spear and sword, an ox for the feast. It would be expensive.

Batian sighed and shifted the little calf again. How could it be heavier now than when they had started to walk in that hour after the sun had reached its highest point in the sky?

The calf was a heifer, smelling pleasantly of milk and the smoke of the fire in the old hut. She was beautifully marked. Her well-shaped head, mostly white, had a distinct star between her eyes, matching the pale fawn shade of the rest of her body. But all of her looked lighter by contrast with Batian's copper-colored skin, so smooth and oiled and sleek, reflecting the sun. Where her head was short-haired, his was closely shaved. She wore no ornaments as yet, but his ears had been pierced, and a bit of smooth ivory hung in the lobe of each one to keep it stretched. Possibly they would reach his shoulders when he was grown to be a morane. He would be tall some day, too, as his sturdy, narrow-hipped frame showed. There was much pride in his dark eyes, and his strong white teeth glistened when he smiled.

Just now Batian was frowning. The little heifer nestled against him trustingly, not minding the thick red dust. But he hadn't thought about food for his charge. And where would he find the mother cow in this crowd of animals, plodding along so close together? When would they stop?

Three things were especially important for their new home. There must be shade and water, grass, too, even though it was drying. And plenty of scrub thorn to build the boma on a flat stretch of ground. Also there must be an old growth of trees to provide saplings for the framework of their huts and poles for the stockade.

A new manyatta must be built, too, after they were settled, where the young warriors-to-be would go to live after the ceremony, separated from their families, though some of their mothers and sisters would keep them company until the girls' marriages could be arranged. His pretty sister Nalo might move from the old one when the time came, and they would see her more often.

Had his father, Ole Kantai, found his mother, Siamanta, that way? He had never thought about that before.

Batian leveled his spear automatically and urged an agile cow back into line. He had done enough herding

A Masai Tribe Goes Walking

since beginning the job a few months before, so that he could work and think at the same time.

The little heifer interrupted his questioning, stirring again in his arm. Surely they had been long enough on the march and would shortly stop? She must be really hungry now. Batian felt like eating, too, but the calf wouldn't want to share his cake of vegetable paste, tied up in his robe. Babies wanted milk and more milk, and this one was so new and so helpless. He was her only protector right now. What could he do?

A warm feeling of responsibility made him hold the calf more closely than he yet had, and her plaintive cry of response roused all the cattle near. The cows that had had calves recently began to moo and push, and all the other herdboys began shouting at their charges.

The women of the tribe had loaded their meager household utensils and bedding on the backs of the family donkeys. The little beasts trudged slowly along under their towering loads. From Batian's place in the line, they could scarcely be seen because of the dust cloud that hovered low. But somewhere among them, with the other women guiding the donkeys and steadying the loads, he knew he'd find his mother, and surely she would be carrying a calabash (gourd) of milk. The only way he could feed such a baby as he carried would be to dip his finger in the milk and let the little thing suck it. He had seen that done often. It was a long and slow process, but if he could find his mother, it would be quicker than to try to locate the mother cow.

The march went on almost another hour while Batian encouraged the little heifer with the sounds that people all over the world use when petting young animals or human babies. His tone of voice, with love in it, didn't need words for expression. Out came a little rough tongue to lick his cheek. What an odd feeling that was, unlike anything he had experienced before. This was the first calf he had been asked to tend.

Little calves were so soft and gentle. When he was a warrior, he'd raise a lot of them and love them all. Now this one must have some milk.

He left his place and walked ahead to find his mother. On the way he heard the loud shout that was the order to halt. It meant that Ole Likimani, the tribe's chief Elder, appointed from Nairobi, and the other two old men who were his associates in managing all tribal matters, had chosen the new place for their boma. Cattle, sheep, goats, donkeys, and people came to a slow stop. The dust began to settle.

Batian's tribe had come to its new home.

2

Siamanta Builds a House

It was strange, Batian thought, that another Masai tribe had not yet discovered the lovely place where his own was now halted. Perhaps they should have walked a little farther the last time, even though that other place had seemed good then.

When the red dust had completely settled, he could see more clearly, far across the backs of the massed animals, how very pleasant this one was.

They had come up a light, tree-shaded rise in the land. From that elevation a vast stretch of grass and scrub growth, full of thornbush, spread on every side, promising some pasturage where the grass wasn't too high, and fencing for the new boma. In the late afternoon sunlight the low hills on the horizon looked almost purple. There was water, too, in a little donga (a stream), which showed by the breadth of its banks that it had room for more volume when the rainy season would begin.

The fragrance of vegetation drying in the hot sun mingled with the odors of the cattle and the stale smell of the cow fat, which all Masai rub on their bodies to keep their fine skin smooth and supple. Batian was used to the fat and the cattle dung. He noticed only the pleasant scent of the drying grasses.

No matter in what direction he turned, the whole prospect was pleasing. Away to the north was the best sight of all, Batian thought. It was the first thing he looked for in the morning and always the last at night, when the sunset colors were reflected so vividly on its snows. That was the towering head of Mt. Kenya. It was said that once, long ago, it had been a higher mountain but that boiling fires inside it had blown the top off. Now there were no longer any flames, only the pure white snow. Someday he would like to climb there and see what the stuff was like. Would it feel soft like the fleece of a baby lamb? Or would it be rough like the hairs of cows when rubbed the wrong way? He had asked and asked, but no one had the answer.

The light had changed a little while Batian stood daydreaming, and now he noticed movement down on the plain and saw what he had missed on first sight. A great herd of zebras and several species of antelope were there, feeding together. Among them were some ostriches, a common sight to Batian. He had seen the great birds often, acting as scouts, giving warnings of lions and wild dogs in the neighborhood.

The slanting sunrays now had caught the glistening black of the zebras' stripes, and the boy was reminded

of another secret ambition, to catch a zebra foal and train it to carry him on its back. The Elders would frown on that. Besides, where could it stay? Not among the cattle in the middle of the boma at night, certainly. They would be restless and keep the whole tribe awake. And later, as it grew, it would be too big to bring into his family's hut.

Batian sighed. The Elders had very strong opinions about so many things. They scorned all animals except cattle, and only tolerated antelope and wild buffalo because their meat tasted most like ox meat, and to eat one of those saved killing a precious animal of their own. Even so, oxen had to be slaughtered occasionally, for ceremonial times like a birth or a wedding, and always for new moranes.

When the boy started on again in search of his mother, he thought that perhaps it wasn't so strange no other Masai people had found this place before. When settled in a new boma, a Masai hadn't much reason to venture far from it. Only at very special times did a journey of any kind call a man away. There was everything he needed at home—milk and blood from the cattle for his staple food, ceremonial roasted meat for all when those occasions occurred, food all about for man and beast, and water. What more was there to be concerned about in a boma if the herdboys did their duty and the cattle were well guarded?

This new place would become home in a short time. It was a part of Masai country, which stretched south from Nairobi town to the border of Kenya and on down into a part of Tanzania. Long ago there had been much more, the Elders said.

Siamanta Builds a House

The noise all about was increasing, but Batian paid no heed. It did not bother him, all the loud talking and laughter and the sounds the animals made. His parents, Siamanta and Ole Kantai, with the other grownups, were planning the positions their houses would have in the new boma. His father would be allowed to choose first because he had more cattle than any other.

The women would build the huts, but they could not begin work until the day after tomorrow. There was a good reason. Everything was done according to old custom. They must wait for a plentiful supply of cow dung to mix with mud for the plaster they used to hold the sapling framework together.

That meant that everybody would sleep under the stars until the huts were ready. For a whole night and a day—tonight and tomorrow—the animals couldn't be taken out to graze. They must stay together in the center of the spot that would be fenced in by woven thornbush.

The late afternoon shadows were growing longer now as Batian slowly made his way in and out among the people and the animals in search of his mother and milk for the little calf. There was no special hurry about anything except hunger at this moment.

Bright-colored birds chattered and chirped in the thorn thickets all about as Batian passed by. If he had not been so close, he wouldn't have heard their lighter notes against the full bellowing of the impatient cattle.

The cows must be milked. The women were waiting to do that after each had been told where her family's hut was to be, just inside the thorn and pole fence that would form the great enclosure. Then she would lead her donkey to the spot and unload there, to mark it. Gourds to hold the milk would be unpacked and the evening fires laid. Those would give warmth as well as add to the other precautions against the possible raid of a lurking lion or leopard.

The fires would be welcomed by all, Batian knew. At this time of year, though the days were warm, the nights might be cool and even cold, and they wouldn't have the shelter of their huts tonight.

Siamanta appeared from behind the towering mound on her donkey.

"Ah, boy, there you are," she said, "just when I need you. Put the little calf down and help me unload."

Batian frowned. "The calf needs milk. I was coming to you for it. Now, please."

His mother smiled, and Batian's frown changed to an answering grin. He was proud of Siamanta. She looked happy all the time. And she was altogether the best-looking woman in the boma, he felt, just as his sister was the prettiest girl. But Batian wanted milk.

"Now," he repeated.

He got another smile and a gesture. "Look about you," his mother commanded. "You will then see that there are many 'nows' waiting. Who is to say which shall come first? A child to order it? My young herdboy? A calf that cannot talk? Or I, builder of houses?"

She stopped teasing him when the frown reappeared and said, "The morning milk is on the load. Help me free the donkey, and I will find it. Then, my herdboy, two 'nows' will be finished, and you may feed the little heifer. She is not complaining. There is time."

Batian nodded and stooped to pat the calf when he

Siamanta Builds a House

laid her on the ground. He talked coaxingly, as if the little thing had protested her hunger loudly. A man had always to show a woman that he was right.

"Those two 'nows' of my mother's must come first, and then you shall see the milk," he promised, and turned to the unloading.

Carefully the woman and the boy together sorted out the variety of things the donkey had borne—some worn blankets, a few homemade clay pots to hold food, and his father's shield. It was a heavy thing of wood and tightly stretched skin, with painted symbols in black and red and white, of significance to the tribe. Now that Ole Kantai was no longer a warrior and did not hunt lions because it was against the law, he did not use his shield. But he had once been a fearless morane before he had married Siamanta, and perhaps, through the shield, his power would one day descend to Batian.

There was a bundle of bullock skins on top of the shield, one for each of the family to sleep on at night, and the tiny stools on which Masai women sat to cook.

Siamanta's chief treasure was packed carefully. It was a small wooden chest, very old, in which she kept copper wire and extra colored beads with which she fashioned the wide collars all the women wore. Sometimes a bead broke and the place had to be mended, or the clasp wore through and another whole wire, which ended in the clasp, had to be replaced. Siamanta herself wore three collars of graduated size, signifying her position as first wife of the wealthiest man in the village.

A long-necked gourd had been propped in the nest of stools. Batian seized it and left his mother to tether the donkey and begin to gather sticks for the fire. His sister should have been there to help with that, but she had been left in the manyatta in the care of her father's mother. The young people were having a dance, and she hadn't wanted to miss it. And she didn't want to work, either, Batian suspected. She might be extra pretty, but along with it she was smart. Boys were expected to work, until they became moranes. Girls had to, all their lives, but his sister was clever at avoiding it. He did not mind working now, not if carrying a calf and tending it as long as it had need was called work.

It was an odd feeling to have his finger sucked so energetically by the little heifer. He first tried holding her jaw open and trickling the milk into her mouth, but she didn't know yet how to eat in any way but sucking, so he gave up and took more time, dipping his finger in the gourd according to custom and thrusting it against the little rough tongue.

Siamanta Builds a House

Fires began to spring up, one by one, as the dusk fell lower, at each position marked for a hut, until there was a steady ring of light around the cattle. They were not massed as closely together now as they had been on the march, and it was easier for each woman to slip in, after identifying her family cows, and take the precious milk.

The men drank their fill of it at night, and in addition to comfort for the cows, that was the next important "now" on any woman's mind. It was in the morning that each owner nicked a vein in the neck of one of his animals and drank perhaps a pint of blood. It did not seem to hurt the beast, and the little slit in a prominent neck vein closed quickly. No one drank from the same animal's supply twice in succession. There was always an interval allowed between times.

That night Batian slept with the calf tucked against him on the skin his mother spread close to the fire. All around them other families were settling down. The moranes who had helped herd the cattle on the march had returned to the manyatta for the dance. They thought nothing of the extra walk, which they would accomplish with their long-legged strides in half the time the cattle and the people had.

By full dark, when the stars were twinkling in their splendor above, the camp was quiet. Far away in the bush a lion roared on a night prowl. Nearby, Batian could hear, with his ear close to the ground, the small scamperings and rustles of tiny creatures as they scurried about on their own searches.

The boy was sure he wouldn't sleep, but after he felt the light fall of a blanket his mother unfolded over him, he knew nothing until morning. The little calf was licking his cheek again, and his mother was planning her day.

"Another 'now' my herdboy," she was saying. "We must go for grain and beans, and you shall carry my basket. There will be nothing for you to do here. And then we will begin cutting the poles and thornbush for the stockade and the houses. We shall build those tomorrow. Up, boy, for your food, and then work."

Batian yawned. It was the usual pattern. Nothing for him had been changed by their move. Nothing but the kind of work, collecting house-building and fence materials instead of herding. That was the only difference. He'd have to find somebody to watch the calf while he was away carrying his mother's basket. Perhaps Soko would do it, or Guhano.

The women made a big thing of their barter and didn't hurry, neither the raisers-of-corn-and-millet nor the Masai mothers of hungry families. They spent much time speculating about how long they would be neighbors and argued about the coming of rain. They couldn't agree on the exact time. It would be when Engai willed it, and that was as far as they got with the weather.

The afternoon provided more diversion for Batian because all the other boys his age had to help collect poles and brush, and they made a game of it.

The building of the huts the next day was dull. There were no games. Each boy helped at his own house. The old men took the cattle out to graze after their long wait, and the shape of the new huts slowly appeared out of the masses of material, after the stockade was formed. The poles and the thorny growth were

Siamanta Builds a House

alternated there in the great circle that outlined the enclosure where people and cattle would live until the next move.

While the Laibon and some of the old men looked on from the comfortable shade of a nearby knoll, and occasionally threw out their ideas of how the work should go on, the women worked steadily and ignored them more than they listened. It was important to finish as fast as possible because the plaster must dry before the huts could be lived in. That meant another night sleeping out under the stars.

The little houses couldn't be built very high since their height, as well as their shape, was determined by the size of the pliable saplings that formed walls and roof. The taller a young tree grew, the stiffer it became above, and the tops of those used had to be bent almost at right angles part way up to form the roof. Five feet to the bend line was not often reached. It meant that grownups couldn't stand up straight inside, but children could.

Batian looked on as critically as the Elders, while he held an armful of saplings and handed them one by one to his mother. Siamanta pushed the lower end of each leafy pole into the ground, following a circle she had marked out, and spaced them apart by the length of her foot. Then she bent the tops over, intertwined them a little to fasten them together, and let all the ends meet in the middle, forming the skeleton structure.

Next she covered the whole framework on top with generous daubs of the overnight cow dung, mixed with thick mud, until the leafy tops of the saplings were hid-

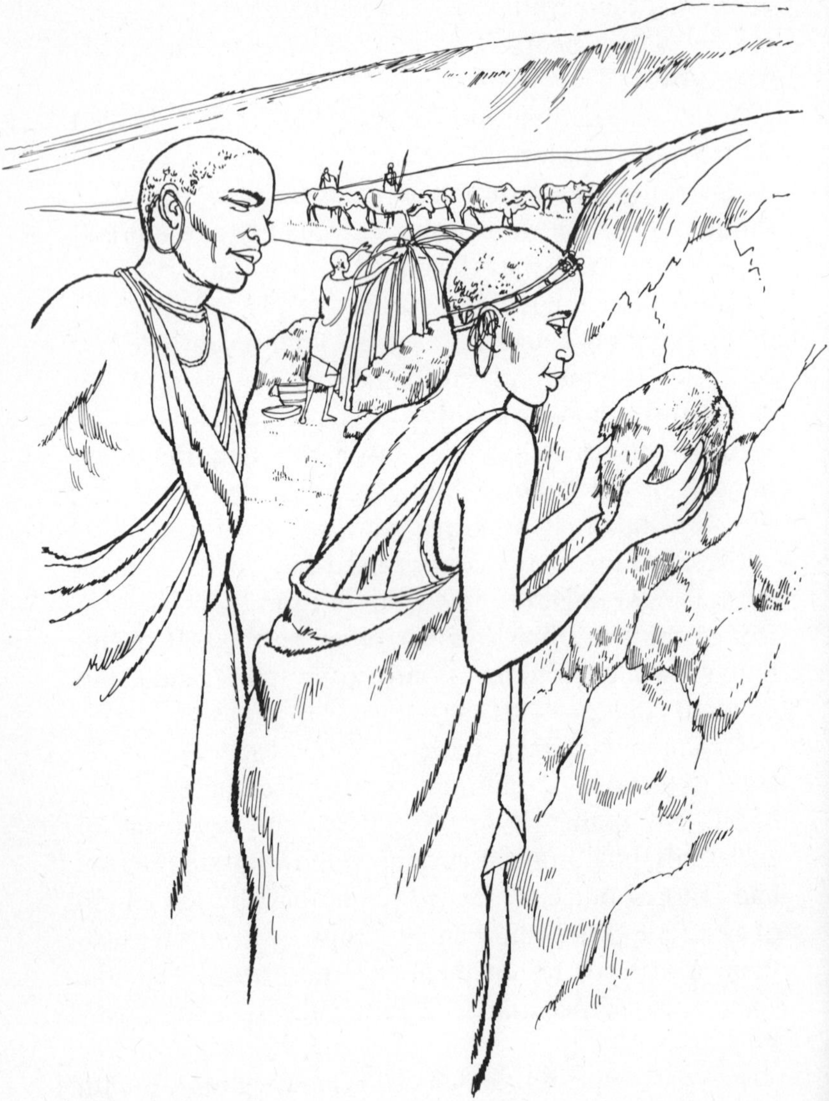

den. Below the roof on all sides the openings between the saplings were filled with mud and leaves kneaded together and covered with the same substance used on the roof. The bend line of the saplings made the corners of the housetop round.

There were places where the plaster oozed and dripped, Batian saw, because his mother had been in a hurry and hadn't made her mixture quite thick enough. But the sun would attend to that, and the whole would be dry and hard after today and the coming night. He had watched such building before and felt he might even do it himself if he were tall enough to reach the roof. Not that any Masai boy or grown man who could reach would ever try to build anything. That was women's work.

Not every builder was as careful as Siamanta, despite her haste, to see that there were openings enough in the center of the roof and near to the places inside where their bed skins would be spread. These were for air to get in and smoke to blow out after the first cooking fire in the center of the floor of the new hut had been lighted.

The only entrance to each of the little houses faced the inside of the boma. It was like a small porch, set out from the wall of the hut a little way at a sharp angle so that anyone entering would turn to the right and stoop to step inside the low-roofed single room. In wet weather bullock hides would be spread above to keep the rain out.

The new hut for Batian's family was located at the right side of their gate on the way into the boma. His father's second wife would live in the one she was building opposite on the left. She was a younger woman and not as skilled as Siamanta. She had several small children, too, and would have fared badly if one of the tribe's grandmothers hadn't helped her.

Batian was glad to be the youngest in his own family. How could he have cared for the little calf as well if he had had to protect it also from the poking fingers of mischievous small children?

The little animal was friskier today. She could stand up on her wobbly legs and butt her hard young head against his knees when he came close enough to the spot where he had tethered her alongside the donkey. He would be glad when they could move all their things into the new hut and keep the calf there safely for a while longer. With so many cattle in the family herds, calves were better off under human protection than with their mothers. It was the custom for kids and calves to be looked after in that way.

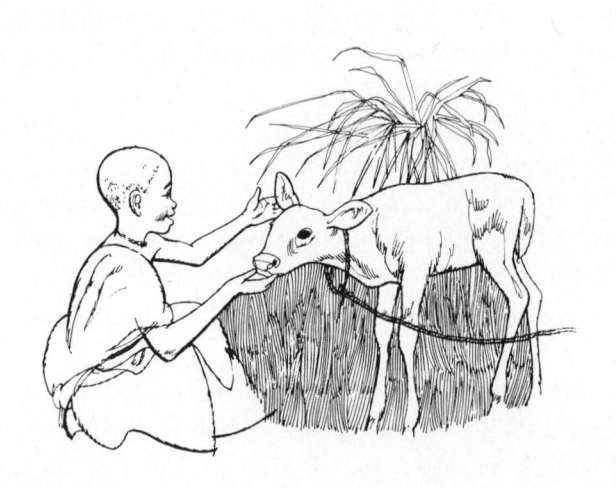

Siamanta Builds a House

Batian watched his mother walk all around the new house when her work was done. The long cloth of a soft red color that draped her whole body from shoulder to ankles was daubed and stained with gobbets of the smelly plaster. Dust from the march still dulled the sheen of her shaved head. But the bright smile was there, and the satisfied laughter as she walked away, with pride in her step.

The boy did not know what she was thinking, the reason for her smile. But it could be, he thought, something about the hut, that she had worked swiftly enough to be among the first to finish. He'd feel that way himself, he decided.

Batian's guess was close.

Once again, Siamanta was thinking, she had built a shelter for her husband and their family. She couldn't count now how many there had been, exactly like this one, since she had fashioned the first, a little clumsily, her bride house. That was after Ole Kantai had come to her father with the bargain price—four worthy-looking cattle and one with a sturdy half-grown calf beside her. The memory was still clear to Siamanta, as if it had happened yesterday and there was still no Nalo and no Batian. How many more huts would she build before the last one—before Engai would let her know that it was time for someone else to make Ole Kantai's roofs?

Batian, watching, saw his mother's smile come and go all day. Siamanta was happy. When her new hut was dry, she would move the family into it, putting the pallets and the stools and the pots in the same places where they had been kept in the hut in the old boma.

As long as they were inside, Batian and his father could feel they had not moved. No, Batian reminded himself, one thing would be different for him. Now he had a calf to tend.

3

The Airplane

The evening fires were lighted a little earlier that night. Their heat would help dry the new huts, and everybody was more tired, at least the women were, than they had been the night before.

When all the cattle had been brought in and the milking was over, the hushed sounds of the end of day died down quickly, though the afterglow of the sunset had not quite faded from the sky.

Batian lay blinking at the stars for a little while, grateful for the warmth of the small calf against his side and for the rough blanket that covered them both.

On the other side of the fire, Ole Kantai lay with his great spear in reach of his hand, in case of any disturbance in the night. He was already snoring gently. That was the only sound nearby except for the stirrings among the animals and the gentle breeze that brushed the leaves of the trees.

Then Batian heard a low humming, far away at first, a sort of singing, but it increased as it came nearer. It was the airplane that they had all seen, many times in daylight, before they moved. The men who flew it seemed to be out very late tonight.

Every Masai in every tribe round about knew that plane and what it was being used for, flying every day over their heads and lands. The men of Batian's people were much troubled that it had come, the Elders most of all.

Batian had heard that there were people in Nairobi town, where a mysterious something called "Government" sat, who said the Masai country was too big and that they should give up some of it. They had what seemed to the boy very strange reasons for their sayings.

One was that the Masai cattle were spoiling the waterholes where the wild animals drank, because their sharp hoofs cut up the soil, and that made the water muddy. Some of the antelopes and lions, the giraffes and zebras were in danger of dying out because of the shortage of the water supply. The Masai shouldn't wander about so much. They also said that some of the grasslands where the wild animals and the Masai cattle roamed together should be given to farmers, who must have new fields to grow crops because there were so many more people in East Africa nowadays and they all needed food.

So, because of all these words, the men in the plane were counting the herds of wild animals and the number of Masai cattle.

Ole Kantai had explained it all to Batian.

Let the lions and leopards and hyenas die out, Ba-

The Airplane

tian thought. Nobody needed them around. Masai cattle had to have water, the same as any other animal did, no matter how their hoofs wore out the ground at the edges of the waterholes.

Ole Kantai had also said that the Masai had friends in Nairobi, as well as enemies. They said that wild animals should be protected from poachers more than from Masai cattle. Poachers were lawless people who killed for money. They took horns from rhinoceroses. They tore off the tails of giraffes and zebras that they snared or shot to make fly whisks. Why bother about flies, Batian wondered. There were lots of them in every boma, but his people did not mind them. Sometimes the poacher-killers left a dead zebra or giraffe on the ground for the vultures and hyenas to eat. Other times they took the skins away also, to sell in Mombasa on the coast of Tanzania. People from the West bought them to spread on their floors. Get after the poachers, not the Masai, said the friendly people in Nairobi, who liked wild animals and wanted them to live.

Batian had asked then, "What do 'they' in Nairobi, that you call 'Government,' think about all the sayings?"

Ole Kantai had looked at his son sadly. He couldn't answer. It seemed that nobody knew yet what "they" would decide.

It was then that he told Batian about another saying in Nairobi that had nothing to do with the Masai's ownership of cattle. That was about their clothing. "The lack of it, rather," Ole Kantai remarked.

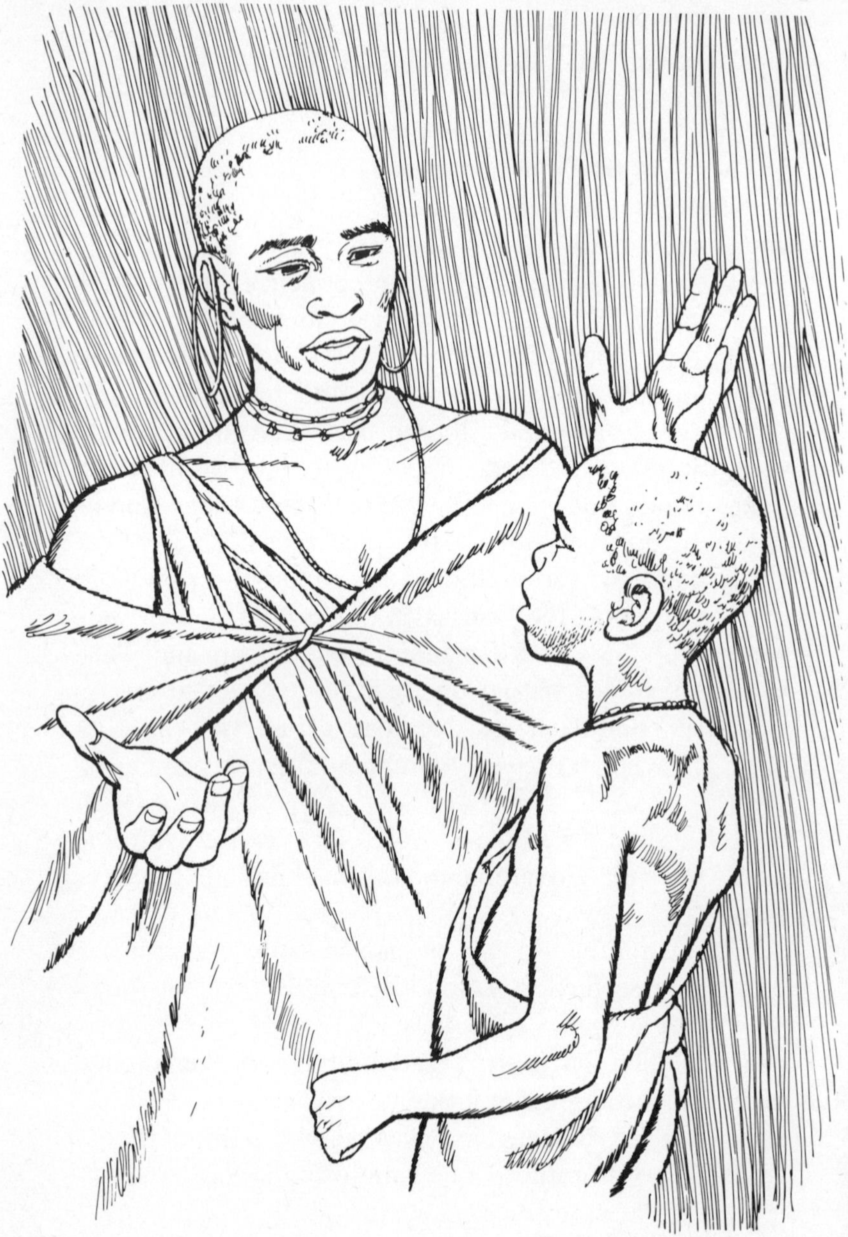

The Airplane

"But we like our way of dressing," Batian had said. "We are comfortable."

"They think we show our skin too much," Ole Kantai answered.

Yet they dressed, as Batian had learned in the Elders' school, in the same way that the tribe had for hundreds of years, except that the women now wore cotton cloth instead of dressed bullock hides. Cloth was one of the few European things that any Masai bought.

"Why have those in Nairobi not spoken before?" Batian asked.

Ole Kantai explained again. "Others' ways have changed, but it is true ours have not. Now the men in Nairobi wear that short, or long, divided garment of Europe that they call 'pants.' They want all in East Africa to do the same. With a shirt on top."

Batian stared at the flickering fire, remembering all his thoughts when he had had that talk with his father. He wondered again how the moranes would look with a garment called "shirt" above those pants. And how would it feel to have a lot of cloth covering one's body? As much as the women and the girls wore. They went about almost completely covered except for one bared shoulder. How would it be for him? Never to feel the direct coolness of the wind after a hot day? Never to know the softness of a lamb's pelt or a kid's when he held one, newborn? The length of red cotton worn on his shoulder and reaching below his knees had its convenient uses, but it was not especially for his protection. Often he took it off to wrap something in it. The moranes wore red-dyed cotton, too, a long strip draped from the right shoulder to the left hip and swinging freely there. Or they wrapped it around their waists, and only their many necklaces covered the bare upper part of their bodies. If cloth was stretched too tightly over one's body, the skin felt scratchy if there wasn't enough cow fat smoothed on.

He remembered asking, "What must we do?"

"Nothing," said Ole Kantai. "We can leave that to the Laibon and to Ole Likimani. Don't worry about it, boy. The cattle come first. That is our concern, not how we look. Oh, the moranes are vain and spend too much time dressing their hair, but look at me. I had the accepted headdress when I was a warrior. But now I have other things to think about, and my shaved head is a comfort. It all lies before you, and for Tipis sooner. Nairobi is some miles away, and what they think and do will be made known to us later. Someday Bolling Bwana will come. I am only telling you what I can, now."

That conversation had taken place some time ago, and Batian forgot the clothing part as he sat up to watch the plane's light, like a moving star, as it circled and went on its way. Had the men flown by to see what their ring of fires meant when it hadn't been there until two nights past? He would pray to Engai that they would be helped to get back to their home safely. That was important to him.

One of his hopes that he had never confided to anyone was to go up and up with those men someday, to ride in their plane among the clouds, to see what they were seeing, no matter what they were using the plane for.

The Airplane

Ole Kantai said that while they counted the kinds of animals, they also were learning where they grazed at different times of the year, the kinds of grasses they liked best, and where they drank water.

And then Batian remembered something from the much teaching he had endured in the Elders' school. Did not everyone know that the Masai were the only great people in the beginning, all one tribe then, and at that time they owned all the cattle in the whole world? That no one else but a Masai had any right to own even one animal? It was a possession that made his people superior to every other race. Therefore, why didn't someone tell those men in the airplane that their work was all for nothing? That cattle came first in East Africa. Lions were meant to be killed so they wouldn't steal Masai cattle for eating.

Batian wished he could waken Ole Kantai right now and ask him why no one had spoken about this to those men in the plane, or to that strange "they" in Nairobi town. His idea ought to help.

The boy couldn't sleep for thinking about the cattle. What would happen to his own hope to build up a great herd for himself after he had been a morane for a proper time, when he would marry and cut off his hair, have a smooth scalp again as he had now?

And how, before that growing up, would a boy, any boy, not only he, Batian, prove he was worthy to become a morane if the decision should go the other way and all the lions should be protected in a reserve and he couldn't kill one? Then he couldn't take its mane to wear in ceremony, proving his skill. Or would lions disappear from Masai country because there were no more cattle for them to kill for food? That could happen in time if "they" in Nairobi decided that the Masai should keep fewer cattle than ever before. Then all his chance for owning as many as he could manage would be gone before he could grow big enough.

Batian thought of all the tender, loving little calves like the heifer that he might never be able to raise. He pulled her warm, soft baby body closer and fell asleep.

4

Visit to the Armorers

Batian was the last of his family to waken on the morning of the day they expected to move into their new hut. He was so surprised that he forgot all of the thoughts the sight of the airplane had brought to his mind the night before.

The little calf was standing up beside him. The blanket that had been so welcome when he went to sleep was now thrown aside because the day was already warming. The fire was only a heap of charred, blackened sticks partly covered by white ashes.

Ole Kantai was calling.

"Waken, boy. We go a-journeying. I need you."

Batian scrambled upright, rubbing the sleep from his eyes. All around the new boma fence the other fires were out, and the cattle were pouring through the gateways, attended by the same old men who had helped with the herding the day before.

It wasn't a usual morning—that was easily seen—and Batian wondered what it meant. How could he have slept through the noise made by the impatient creatures through the tick search? This was the third morning since the tribe had left the burning boma to come to this place. The cattle weren't used to it yet. They hadn't liked being penned up a full night and a day and another night before they could try out the new pasture.

What was the meaning of the coming journey? Were only he, Batian, and his father going? And what would he do with the little calf?

O-ho, she could stay in the new hut with Siamanta. It was only then that Batian noticed their household things had disappeared. All the sleeping skins had been picked up except his. The stools and the cooking pots were no longer stacked beside the thorn fence. The women had begun moving inside.

Siamanta came hurrying with Batian's morning food, steaming in a small wooden bowl. She had made a hot mixture of fat and ground corn that he especially liked, a substantial meal. That meant, very possibly, that the coming journey, whatever its object, would not be a short one.

The boy ate hungrily while his father talked.

"This is the day we go to the armorers," he said. "We will bring back Tipis's new spear and sword."

"How did you remember that this was the day?" Batian asked. He knew that the order had been given some time ago, before they had had to move. They were farther away now from the Ol Kunoni, those Masai who worked in iron and other metals. This journey would take longer than it had the first time.

Visit to the Armorers

"I didn't remember, exactly," Ole Kantai admitted. "I think the Ol Kunoni said to come back in eight days, or perhaps it was ten. I don't know, but we will go, anyway. If we are already late there, it is better that we go now. We should be prepared and ready when the Laibon finds that the right time has come to hold the new moranes' celebration. It could be any day now."

"Then what made you think of it this morning?" Batian persisted as he held the bowl up to his mouth to get the last bit of liquid.

"Every morning after the order for Tipis's spear and sword was given, your mother took a blue bead out of her box and dropped it into this little gourd." Ole Kantai held it up for Batian to see. "And she meant to put the right number in, but when the old man died in the boma and we had to move, she forgot, and the gourd wasn't found until this morning when she cooked the ground corn for you. It was in a pot she hadn't yet used here. There were only six beads in it, and she can't remember how many more should be with them. So now we will go, and I want you to come with me to choose the animals we will take to the Ol Kunoni for payment. Tipis and his father will be with us. The things are for him, so he must touch them first."

"And the other four boys and their fathers? They, too?" Batian asked, setting his bowl down reluctantly. He'd have liked another helping, but his father noticed and shook his head.

"There is meat prepared for me to take on the walk. I will give you some of it if you are hungry on the way. I cannot drink milk tonight if I eat meat in the daylight, but meat is easier carried than milk. Come. Let us choose the animals, which will not be difficult. Of course the other boys and fathers will be with us. All must be ready for the ceremony together."

Batian counted on his fingers the number who would be walking with them as he and his father went down onto the plain to find their own animals and make the selection for payment to the armorers. There would be five new warriors and their fathers, and he and his father extra because Ole Kantai was providing Tipis's equipment. Surely the Laibon would come, too? One of the three Elders? No, they liked the comfort of a shade tree near the boma on a hot day. But the Laibon's oldest son, who was training to be a medicine man, would probably come. That many people.

And the number of animals? They would be chosen according to the price each father was willing or could

Visit to the Armorers

afford to pay. A bullock for a fine spear, and something less or not as good for the sword.

No matter what was offered, the Ol Kunoni would be obliged to accept, even though their spears and swords were always made of first quality. Their work was beautiful, but they were not allowed to bargain about payment. Only inferior people worked with iron and fire. Iron was found in the ground and had no life in it. Therefore, it was considered unclean. That was why the soon-to-be moranes must go to the Ol Kunoni boma to receive their new weapons. They would carry oil and rub it on their hands before touching anything an armorer had handled in the fashioning. Only the fat prevented the spear from working some kind of harm for its new owner.

Why didn't bad things happen to the armorers themselves when they worked the iron they found in the ground or bought from the traders coming in from the coast? Batian had asked that question in the Elders' school and had never been satisfied with the answer he was given. Someday he would know, the teacher said, though he might have to wait until he himself would possibly become an Elder, but there was plenty of time in life to find out everything that was necessary to know. The Elder's face was stern, and Batian hadn't dared to ask why he had to wait so long to find out what he'd like to know now.

One of the old men herders had separated the sheep from the cattle, and Ole Kantai looked at his own flock critically. He selected an old ram with a crooked horn and a ewe that limped. Her fleece was dirty and full of seed burrs, and one eye was gone.

Batian watched and to his own surprise shook his head in protest. "It is not good to choose these," he said.

His father had said they would make the choice together. Hadn't he meant it?

Ole Kantai's remark was brusque. "It is the custom to get rid of poor stuff this way," he said. "Nothing more."

Batian was encouraged. "But my cousin Tipis will be shamed before the other moranes, won't he, if the animals their fathers take along are better?"

The man laughed harshly and then stared at his son. "What kind of thinking is this?" he asked. "Tipis ashamed? His sword and spear will be equally good with the others'. Why should the payment matter?"

His tone told Batian that he felt his choice of animals to pay for the weapons had nothing to do with Tipis's feelings. After that Batian knew he ought to keep still, but he couldn't and was ready to argue further.

Then Ole Kantai said, "The armorers do not expect first quality for their payment. The things they make are their way of life, as ours is to raise cattle. They were born to the iron working as were we to herding. They know they are an inferior people. Why should they be given the best animals?"

By that time Batian had begun to feel a little frightened for speaking to his father as he had, but he answered bravely.

"I was not thinking of the armorers, my father, but of my cousin Tipis's pride. That's what they teach in the Elders' school—goodness to our fathers and moth-

Visit to the Armorers 55

ers and brothers and sisters. The armorers were not mentioned when that was said."

He could not explain his feeling that Tipis would dance better at the celebration and yell louder and dare to make up to a pretty girl if he knew that his uncle had given a fine lot of animals for his equipment. It would be different if Tipis's own father had paid for his spear and sword. Tipis was a strong, proud boy.

Ole Kantai looked at Batian wonderingly for a moment. Then he grinned at the boy and said, "You speak somewhat truly, though I have never heard such twistings of thought as yours. I, too, was taught generosity to my family, long ago, when I was young, but I did not then get the same meaning."

He gestured to the herder, rejecting his first choice of payment and went on to the cattle.

Batian felt proud when the men and boys began the journey. He herded a fine black bullock, quite young, not a white hair showing on his sleek hide, the sort that was usually reserved for ceremonial feasts. He had a black nanny goat with one kid as black as she. He had a black cow with four white feet. It was the best selection of animals that any father had ever made for the occasion, the boy was sure.

The other men looked wonderingly at the three fine animals and then at Ole Kantai and back to Batian, but none was brave enough to ask any questions as they trudged along the dusty road.

Their way led back over the miles they had traveled to the new boma, and the Ol Kunoni were some distance beyond it. They saw that the roofs of the huts where they had once lived had fallen in because of the fire and knew that after the coming rainy season all would have broken down so completely as to become a part of a landscape round and about. They hurried past, afraid that the old man's spirit might still be hovering nearby.

At the manyatta where the older moranes of their tribe lived, they stopped briefly to visit with Batian's sister, Nalo. She was pleased to see the four members of her family, but she didn't ask about the new boma. Her life in the manyatta now absorbed her whole thought.

On leaving Nalo, they had only two more miles to travel before they would come to the Ol Kunoni village.

It was lovely land they walked through, even on a hot day in the dry season. The low hills were dim outlines behind the shimmering heat waves that rose in the sunlight. A lion and his pride looked down on them sleepily from the height of a great ant heap where bushes had taken root and shaded them. At a farther distance a herd of giraffes, their cream and brown

Visit to the Armorers

coats almost unseen against the trees, nibbled from the top leaves. And always above them, far away, was the gleaming peak of Mt. Kenya.

All around, the pasturage was growing higher and drying out. It wouldn't be long before it would have to be burned off everywhere because Masai cattle wouldn't eat tall grass. There was no nourishment in the top joints of the stems. But how they loved the juicy new growth that appeared on the blackened earth after one of those ground fires and the first heavy rain.

There was movement in a patch of high growth just

before they reached the Ol Kunoni, and they saw what caused it as they came a little closer. A group of perhaps twenty crowned cranes was feeding on the seeds. They wore capes of dark blue feathers on their backs and had white waistcoats under lacy lemon-yellow feathers low on the sides. A drooping sober brown tail extended far below those white waistcoats, and high up, above all the splendid blending of shades, their red wattles showed beneath the golden crown plumage.

Batian looked back after their little company had passed the birds, wondering how he might snare one. He had heard they could be tamed, but no one in his boma had ever tried. They thought only of cattle. Some of the young warriors liked to decorate themselves with bright-colored bird feathers, but who could dream of killing one of these beautiful creatures? Yet how could he manage to have one as a pet, no, two, because one would be lonely without a mate, if he should later have several calves to tend at the same time? He sighed and turned again to watch the road.

The Ol Kunoni armorers were ready for them. All the men and women came out to watch the transaction.

The boys oiled their hands before they touched anything the armorer men had made. They rubbed the shafts of their spears with the shining fat and walked around making lunging motions to test their new weapons for weight.

Just before the circumcision rites, the boys had been allowed to let their hair grow, and by the time they celebrated their coming of age as warriors, it would be ready to braid into many little plaits, which would

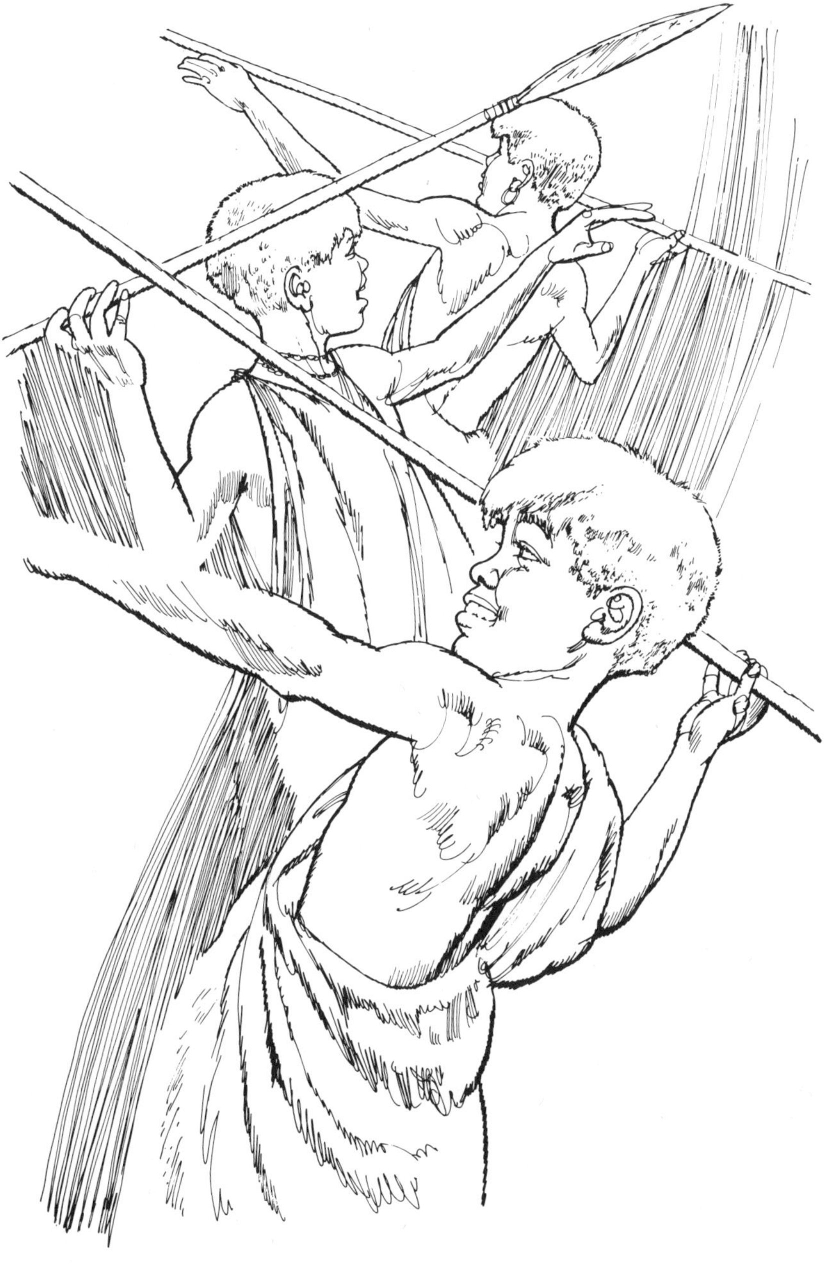

then be separated into sections and plastered to their heads with fat and red clay mixed together.

Now, as they tried out their spears, the fluffy new hair blew about, and they self-consciously tossed it out of their eyes as they leaped up and down.

There were many pleased grins when the craftsmen saw the quality of the three black animals Ole Kantai offered them. They even lost their worried, humble look for a few minutes.

The business was almost over when Batian discovered a row of cowbells set out on a board near one of the armorers' houses. Usually they made big ones, suitable to be used around the neck of a full-grown herd leader. But this smith had made some smaller ones, too, and Batian coveted one to tie on the neck of his heifer. He drew his father over to the display and pointed out the one he would choose if he could have it. He didn't ask for it aloud. Ole Kantai understood.

There was no bargaining for the bell. The armorer said that because they had brought such good animals in payment for Tipis's spear and sword, Batian could have the one he wanted.

He was about to pick it up when he felt a warning hand on his shoulder. Tipis was there, handing him some of the oil he had brought to use in claiming his spear. After he had used it, he could claim his gift. It had a pleasant, tinkling sound. Now he would always know where his calf was when he heard it.

Because they did not have to herd the animals on their way home, nor fit their pace to the plodding creatures, they took less time to return to the new boma.

The new young warriors, moranes to be, carried

Visit to the Armorers

their spears proudly and were teased by their fathers. Batian heard it all, but his thoughts were a mixture of crowned cranes, the lovely color on the hills as the afternoon sun lowered, and the new bell.

What would the three Elders say when they heard the story of the way Batian had talked to his father? He had only acted on their teaching, and the Masai were known to be kind to each other and generous to their families when they had the means. It was puzzling. He knew more than he had last year or the year before. Was that the way he would someday know everything? More each year? Was that why the tribe was willing to be ruled by what their Elders decided for them, because the old men knew more than anyone?

He drew a deep breath of satisfaction. That was a new thing he had learned all by himself today. His feet lagged. He was tired. It would be good, when they reached home, to eat another meal, and then he could lie down with the little calf on his pallet and sleep. But tonight he wouldn't see the stars. He wouldn't be able to search for the Pleiades and count them. The tribe believed that the six stars they could see were cows, watching over all the cows on earth. The roof of Siamanta's new hut would shut out the sky.

They were within perhaps a half mile of home when Batian heard again the distant sound that would come nearer and nearer and there would be that airplane, hovering above them. It was on its way back to Nairobi probably, returning earlier than last night. There was a lovely light in the sky now. The sunset was turning Mt. Kenya's peak to some of the crowned cranes' bright colors.

All the men stopped to look at the plane, and then it zoomed down, closer and closer, and one of the fliers waved before it climbed steeply into the sky again and was gone.

The little group talked about the startling sight all the rest of the way home. They were not expecting the welcome they received there. All of the people were out, watching the road as the men and boys struggled along toward the various gates in the thorn fence. It was clear that something exciting had happened in their absence. The families were not interested in the new spears the boys carried—not a bit of it. They had news of their own, but everyone shouted so loudly that separate words could not be understood at first.

It was not until the Laibon held up his hand and the people were still that the homecomers discovered what the excitement was.

It seemed that the airplane had touched down at the boma in midday and the men had talked to the Elders. And they were returning tomorrow. Possibly some of them would be taken into the sky for rides. One of the men had been Bolling Bwana, their District Officer.

The smallest children were crying and holding to their mothers' skirts as if they never meant to let go. Batian went to his father's other wife's little ones and rang his new bell for them, but they wouldn't look at it. They even yelled a little louder.

"Why are they afraid? What makes them cry?" he asked.

Siamanta picked up the baby boy and petted him. She said, "They understand about the rides in the sky, even this baby. They are afraid the plane will go away

Visit to the Armorers

and take Ole Kantai in it, and they will never see him again. The Bwana said that those who ride up will become birds and fly, too."

It couldn't be true, Batian reflected, and then because Siamanta was laughing, he laughed, too, so hard that the baby boy stared at him and then reached for the bell.

What silly things babies could be made to believe!

Underneath the laughter his heart was thumping painfully. Would the Bwana take any boys up? Was it only to give rides that they were coming again? Was the time so near when one of his own hopes would come to pass? Could he sleep tonight, though he was so tired?

5

Boma Meeting

It took the whole boma longer than usual to settle down that night. Even the cattle were restless. They had caught the feeling of excitement from the people.

Batian lay sleepily quiet on his pallet, stroking the little calf's forehead while he listened to the talk of his father and mother.

Siamanta was telling again the incidents of her afternoon, everything she herself had noticed about the visit of the District Officer, whose business it was to supervise the Masai. The young British pilot of the light plane they traveled in was with him.

"Bolling Bwana asked for Ole Likimani," she said. "You know the Bwana speaks our words, so we understood and were not afraid."

"Did they say why they had come?" Ole Kantai asked.

"I did not hear that," said Siamanta.

"And afterward?" Ole Kantai urged.

"Bolling Bwana went to the tree on the knoll that I

Boma Meeting

pointed out and talked to the Elders a long time," Siamanta said.

"And you do not know what they talked about?"

"I did not say that."

From the tone of his mother's voice, Batian knew that she was smiling in the dark.

"Then you did listen?" Ole Kantai was surely grinning.

"All the women did. Was that bad?"

Ole Kantai laughed aloud. "You know it wasn't, that we'd want to have your story when we came home. Speak, woman."

Batian could hear then his mother's soft sighs. "Land, my husband. Always it is about the land. Because we move around and the cattle spoil the waterholes for the wild ones who come to drink, too. And that we have too many cattle, and there are too many people in the Masai country now. They want to chop some of it up and put seeds in it, to make more food for those who eat differently from our way. We did not understand. The Masai have always lived here, where we can see Mt. Kenya, or farther south in the Serengeti. Why are they making trouble now?"

Ole Kantai yawned deeply. "Sleep, woman. We will do nothing, and they can't do anything. In Nairobi they worry now about the land and the animals. Tomorrow it will be something else. There will not be trouble. It is only that Bolling Bwana has to do his work."

Siamanta protested. "But they talked of schools. How can we send our children to a school far off to learn others' ways? And wear clothes like theirs? Our young ones won't know where to find us when the school does not keep . . . not all the year, he said."

"Who said?"

"The Bwana."

"But what have schools to do with land? They were talking of our Masai country, you say." Ole Kantai was puzzled.

"They talked about both. There must have been a reason," said Siamanta.

Ole Kantai rolled over, ready for sleep. "Enough, woman, this that I have heard," he commanded. "The Elders know how to teach our children. Be at peace."

Batian's last thought before he, too, fell asleep was to wonder how he might be invited to go up in the airplane if he had to be out herding the cattle the next morning. He couldn't be present to push into the front row of the boma welcomers.

When he woke, he found that that morning would again be different from their usual ones. While the rest of the boma had slept, Ole Likimani and the other two Elders who helped him manage all their affairs had decided to call a meeting. And the children were to attend, so some of the older men, grandfathers, were obliged again to herd the cattle that day.

Batian listened to the order with a satisfied smile. No matter what would be said at the meeting, he could now be present when Bolling Bwana came back in the plane.

He watched the cows and the sheep and the goats pushing through the gates in the thorn fence, anxious to get to the pasture land, though it was daily growing more dry and the grass stems higher. Rain must come

Boma Meeting

soon. Maybe the women should pray harder. It didn't seem, this morning, that anyone was thinking of Engai. They were too excited, so anxious to be the first to hear the plane coming.

Ole Likimani and his companions had drawn apart under the tree on the knoll, their favorite spot, become so in these few days, where presently all the boma would join them and listen to their words. Why did they want all the young herdboys present? Must they have a meeting on this very morning when there was so much else to think about?

Batian pondered that question while he attempted to string his new bell on a small bit of leather thong so that he could fasten it around the heifer's neck. He had just finished when the signal came for the people to gather, so he thrust his hand through the crude necklace and led the calf with him.

Siamanta was with Ole Kantai's other wife, helping her tend the babies, so she did not need her son and his pet for company.

"And I can go about by myself now," the boy thought. The realization was a little startling. Maybe his mother had thought of that. She had not ordered him to stay on the ground if he should be invited to ride up into the sky. Maybe she didn't think he would get the chance. No matter. He would decide for himself when the time came, if it should, but they'd have to let him take the calf back to the hut first. Yet, if he was out of sight that long, some other boy might get his place. What should he do?

The people gathered quietly on the Elders' knoll. They had chosen a fine place where they could oversee

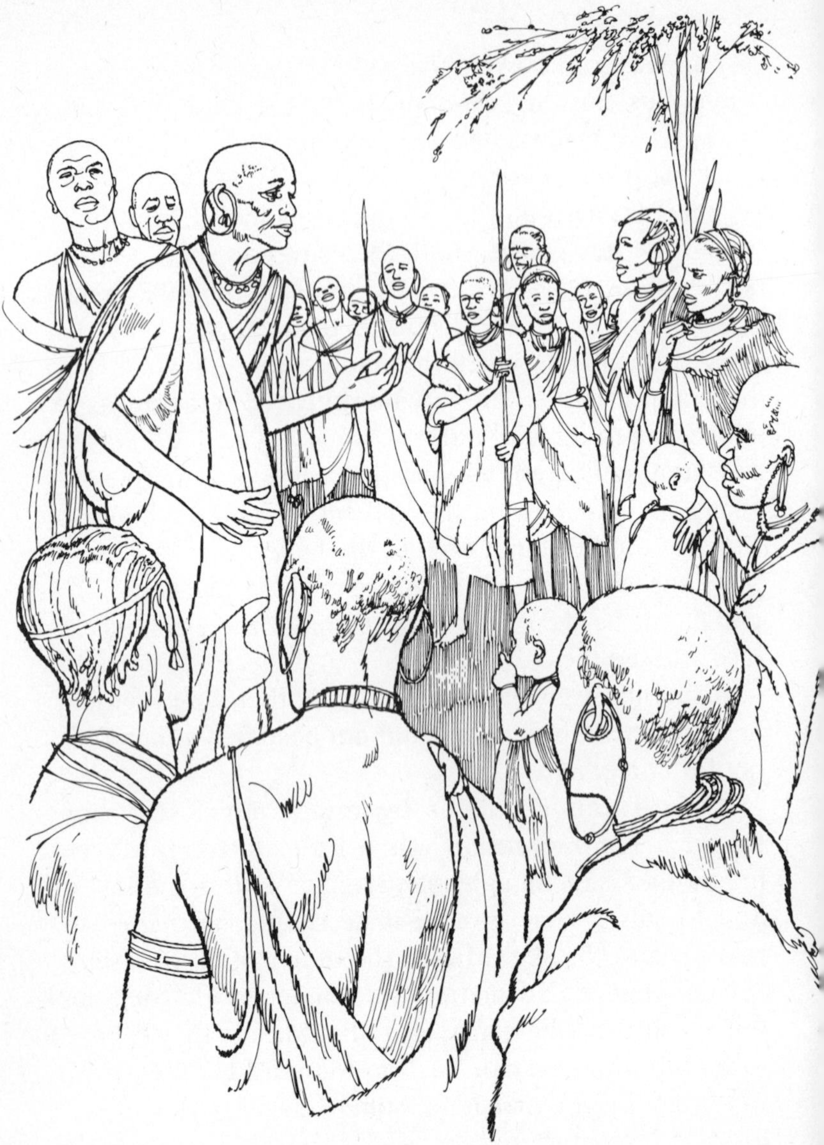

Boma Meeting

all that went on in and around the boma. The old men looked stern this morning, and the mothers hushed the whimpering babies.

Ole Likimani began the talking.

"The Bwana came yesterday," he said, "while some of you had business with the Ol Kunoni. He had much to say. We listened. We had heard most of it before. Our herds are spoiling the waterholes. The Masai in the Serengeti Plain and that great crater called Engorongoro are pressing for our rights as original owners of all this country, given us by Engai. If they at Nairobi and Mombasa give back to us some land that is already ours, they say it will endanger the life of the wild animals that live part of the year there. They also say it is not good for people to live where wild animals wander. Now, he said, the time has come for action."

The people waited for Ole Kantai to speak. He asked, respectfully, "What kind of action?"

"Possible forcing of our people to keep smaller herds, though he says they will then be better because there will not be enough room on the land for all we have now if more crops are allowed. Already some are planting seeds without permission. Nairobi will give us sprays and the work of animal doctors to keep our herds healthy. Some of you have seen the value of this, though you refuse it for this tribe." Ole Likimani looked very solemn as he spoke.

Tipis's father said, "The Bwana is appointed to be our friend. How is it that he comes with such words now? The old Masai ways were good for us. We do not like change."

There were murmurs from the other men. They

wanted more explanation. The women were silent, though they exchanged knowing glances. They were not expected to speak. They could only listen.

Ole Likimani said, "My brothers, the Bwana knows more because he hears talk that we do not. He says we should make our herds smaller, or the time may come when they will eat away so much grass that there will not be enough for all on the land that is not made into fields. The Bwana says also that if your herds are better cared for because of the medicines you will be given, you will live just as well with fewer animals."

Ole Kantai said, "But think of the bride wealth we have to pay for our wives, and the animals for the Ol Kunoni for spears, and those we have to kill for feast days. We need many cattle."

The Elder nodded. "I have thought of those things, all the night," he said. "The Bwana said more, this time."

Again there was a murmured response. Now it expressed surprise and curiosity together.

Ole Likimani lifted his hand and gestured to the Elder on his right. "Tell them," he said, "what the Bwana thinks might help, though it will take time."

The crowd was silent. The people could see that the second Elder was hesitating. He did not want to speak. Ole Likimani looked annoyed, and finally he himself said just one word.

"Schools."

The tribe was puzzled. They had them, their own, to teach the children Masai history and legends. They needed nothing more.

The old man went on then, as if he had read their thinking.

Boma Meeting

"We have our own. That is true. But the Bwana says they are no longer enough. Our children must know more. There are schools for them in Nairobi and down near Engorongoro Crater, where they learn things that will help them work for our people's good later. It is no longer enough that our babies know our legends. We need them, when they grow up, to help us fight for our rights—fight with equal knowledge, so that we may keep our lands and our old ways as we have always tried to do. Now that other Masai tribes have begun sending their children to schools out in that other world, why should we not do so also?"

The people looked at each other and were silent, no murmur rising to express anything. They were not sure they had understood Ole Likimani. He did not often make such long speeches. Schools? When? How could a boy go to one of those places and still become a morane? What would happen to that old custom?

Batian was as bewildered as the grownups. He had already thought of some of these things, but he could not tell anyone how great his fears had been.

And then they heard the plane, coming in for a landing. They had not been aware of its far-off, approaching sound. They had been listening too hard to the talk from the knoll. And nothing had been decided. Why had Bolling Bwana said he would come back this morning? Did he expect an answer as to what they would do that fast? He couldn't, when he knew that it wasn't Masai custom to hurry. Their habit was to talk and talk before they decided anything.

Batian got up from his place on the ground and found his mother beside him. On her left arm she held the baby boy from his father's other hut. With her right hand she was reaching for the heifer's neck thong. Her eyes were shining.

"I will take the calf with me," she said. "Hurry, my herdboy. Haven't you guessed what Bwana Bolling wants? It is not the Elders who will be given rides, nor the men, your father and Tipis's and the others, nor even the soon-to-be moranes. He knows who they are. It is the younger boys such as you. He wants to see what you are like. A thing he said yesterday is now quite clear to me. Run. Get up in front, so you will be asked to fly up in the air. You've wanted it. Now it can be true."

The boy let the calf's bell leather slip out of his hand while he hesitated, looking at Siamanta. How did she know? He hadn't spoken to anyone of his great hope. But she must know. How else could she have spoken as she had just now? Though they didn't allow the women to say a word at meetings, she must have caught more meaning than the others yesterday. H'm.

He turned away with a nod to her and was off, dodging in and out among the hurrying, pushing people, so as to be first on the spot where Bolling Bwana and his pilot were stepping out of the light plane.

6

Sky Ride

As he ran, Batian knew that other herdboys were following him. And when they reached the plane, he saw that several of those who ran with him would one day be in the same "age-set" of young moranes as he. They'd be fifteen at about the same time.

But if they should be sent to that school near the great crater far in the south, beyond the Kenya border, how could they ever be moranes? He was annoyed that that uneasy thought should come now, and he dismissed it in the pleasure of the moment. Would he be chosen to fly?

When all the running boys drew up in a panting row in front of Bolling Bwana, the big man bowed to them, paying no attention to the grownups of the boma who were crowding around.

When he spoke, he used their own Masai words. "I will take you and you and you," he said, indicating Batian and Soko, one of his best friends, and one other. Batian was sorry that Guhano, also a close friend, had not run faster. Maybe he could go up the next time. The Bwana had watched them coming, and his choice had been fair.

"And I will show you a truth that is to be seen from the sky, and you will tell it to all the others when you come back," said the Bwana, motioning them toward the door of the plane.

At that a great chorus of "Ahs" rose from the listeners, the surprised grownups, who did not see why boys should be preferred, and the disappointed boys who had not been chosen.

The three fortunate ones were so excited that they were clumsy climbing into the plane. Their small spears got in the way. No one suggested leaving them behind because they wouldn't be needed. That would never occur to any Masai male, whatever his age. Once received, his spear became a part of him.

Nor did the District Officer offer to help by holding a spear while the owner stepped in and settled into place inside. He knew his touch would be frowned on. So he waited patiently, and when the door was shut, before the pilot moved the stick, he spoke to the boys again, still in that clear Masai speech they understood so well.

"Up in the sky I cannot talk to you easily because the plane makes a loud noise. You could not hear me, I think, so hear me now. I want you to see your Masai lands, so we'll go first to Nairobi town, a place you have only heard about."

The surprised boys looked at each other. Those left behind also hoped for rides today, many, for a few minutes. That was how the plan had been understood.

Sky Ride

Now the Bwana's idea seemed different. On foot, Nairobi was known to be a long distance away. Of course in the plane, it would take much less time. Anyone could see that. But the boys were uneasy.

Batian spoke for all three. "What about all those others?" he asked anxiously. "We thought . . ." and then he stopped, helplessly.

The Bwana waved his hand carelessly. "There will be plenty of time for them someday," he said. "So I have spoken to Ole Likimani. It will be explained."

So this wasn't going to be a short trip up among the clouds, just to show three Masai herdboys how it felt to fly and what the earth looked like from up there. Was the Bwana speaking true? It could be that this very morning he was taking them to that school near the great crater and they'd never see their new boma, or any other, again. No, he was not lying. He had said they would return.

In the moment of reassuring himself, Batian realized he must help the other two if they had fears. But why had three boys been chosen to fly to Nairobi? Why not some fathers, those who had sons about to become moranes? All of the tribe would have seen that as honor to them.

When the Bwana nodded to the pilot, the young man drew the stick back. The three passengers watched his hand so closely that they did not know they were rising from the ground until they saw they were above the treetops, so high that they could look down on a tall giraffe, stretching its neck to get a mouthful of acacia leaves.

Where was the boma?

It had disappeared, but far ahead was Mt. Kenya, its shining beauty familiar and loved. Batian settled back in his seat, glad now that he had been chosen for this journey.

Between the plane and the mountain there appeared a great herd of wildebeest and zebras and some kinds of antelopes, and the pilot flew a little lower so that they could get an even better look. The animals seemed to know as much as the Masai did, that even in the dry season grass stayed fresh longer on the higher slopes.

Off to one side there was a small group of little gazelles called *Tommies,* whose tails went constantly round and round. Batian loved to watch them and had asked if their tails ever stopped moving when they were asleep. But no one could answer him.

The presence of the herd made Batian think of the talk of the morning. Why had there been lately so much said about four things together—the wild animals, the Masai cattle, the water, and the land? Surely there was enough of the bush and grassy plains for all, and there seemed too many wild ones to fear they'd ever die out. It appeared that way now, looking down.

And then, beyond the place where the animals grazed, something, a truly strange sight, began to spring up right out of the ground and grow taller as they approached. The white mass, shining white in the sun, separated into parts of different heights. What were they? A different sort of boma?

The Bwana turned in his place and motioned with his hand, making sure that they were looking in the right direction, and the pilot flew still lower. Were they

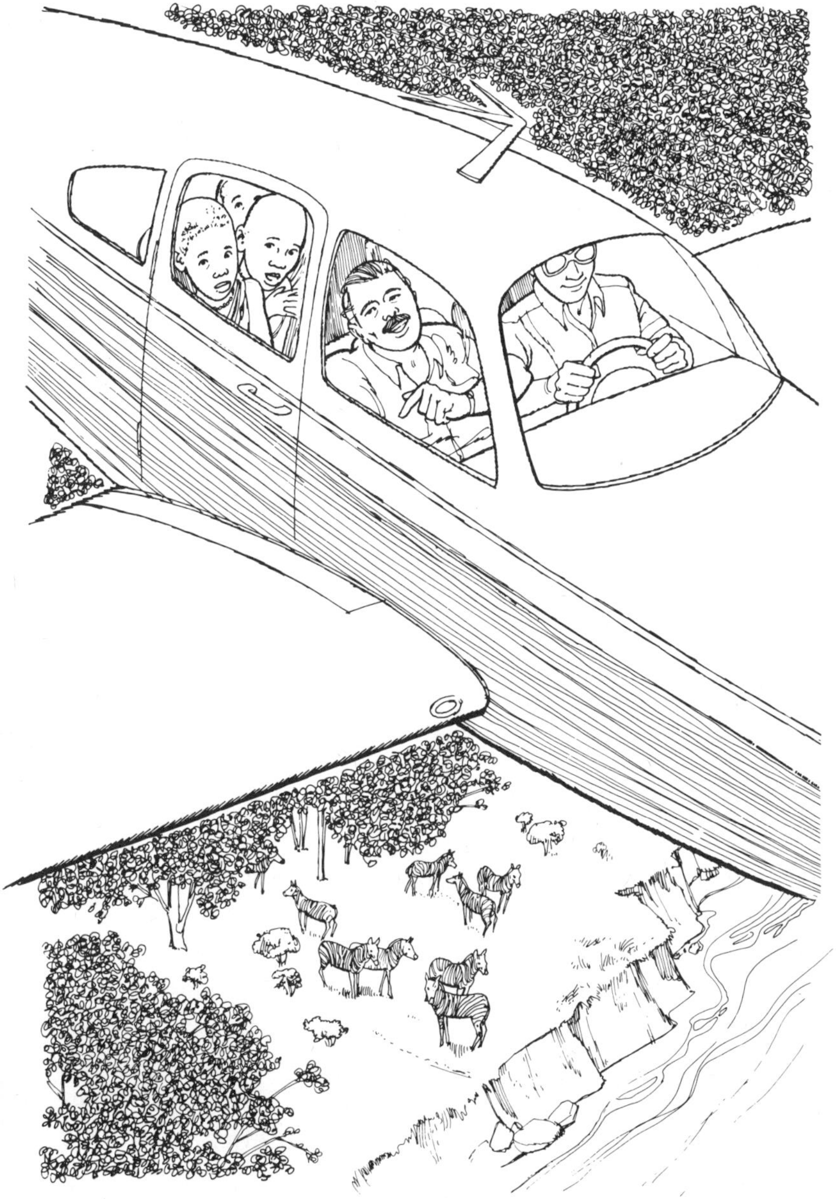

coming all the way down to the ground? Was this place that school? No, it couldn't be, because the old Elder had said that the crater school was in the south, away from their beautiful mountain.

Soko shut his eyes and clutched Batian's hand. "Engai, Engai," he muttered, and Batian knew that his friend was afraid.

The plane came down gently, rolled a little and stopped, and that ended the noise inside it. Soko opened his eyes, but kept tight hold of Batian's hand. They could hear the Bwana talking once more.

"This is Nairobi town," he explained, "where Kenya's Elders and some younger men make the laws for all of us."

Batian had a feeling of satisfaction. Now he knew who were the mysterious "they" who said the good and bad things about the Masai.

The three boys stood huddled together while the Bwana and his pilot talked in *Waingereza* (English) as it was called in Swahili and used by all Europeans. Batian listened closely but couldn't understand a single word. Any talk sounded very strange when not in Masai or Swahili, that other tribal language that Batian and his people knew and used when necessary.

The pilot turned back to the plane, and Bolling Bawana led his three guests some distance away to a strange-looking object that appeared to be a box on wheels—a box of a very odd shape indeed. The boys had seen jeeps once in a while when Europeans came to take pictures of zebras and giraffes. But this wheeled thing of the Bwana's was the queerest they had yet seen. He had to practically lift each one of

Sky Ride

them inside it, and they sat down gingerly on the thick white cloth that covered the seats. How did one breathe in such a box when the door was shut?

The Bwana sat behind a wheel, and when he set his hands on it, the box began to move. One did breathe quite easily, they found, and after a while they saw that there was no cloud of red dust coming in to settle on their heads and their smooth copper-colored skin.

"The pilot will stay with the plane," said the Bwana, "while I show you where Kenya's Elders sit in their Council Hall."

The ride into the city was short. Soko forgot to be afraid because there was so much to see, strange people in stranger clothing, and there were portions of the street meant only to be walked on. And many more boxes on wheels went by, just like the one they sat in. Their respect for the Bwana increased. It must be something very high and honored to have such a moving box.

They got out of the car in a wide street and left it, locked, when they crossed a sidewalk and went through a tall door into a taller building. Then, inside another great door they found a room with carved wood paneling, where many men sat on benches and listened to another one talk.

"So they really did sit to make the laws," Batian thought, and promised himself he would remember to tell Siamanta that.

The place where they were standing was very crowded when they first entered the Council Hall. But after a while Batian noticed that the space around them was growing larger and larger. People, who seemed to be visitors as were they themselves, were staring at the boys, and he heard the word "Masai." That was all he understood. But the woman who spoke put a small piece of white cloth over her nose. She looked angry.

Batian knew they were saying something bad about his people. So now he had seen some of those enemies that his father had talked about. The Bwana's face was growing very red, and in a moment he was hurrying them out through both the fine doors and into the street.

Something was wrong, but the Bwana still did not say anything while he made the little motorcar go very fast out to the airport.

The pilot stared at them when they arrived and spoke in the Masai tongue to ask why they had come back so soon.

Bolling Bwana looked at the boys, and his face got red again before he explained everything in their own speech. But it was even then difficult to understand what was wrong because there were no words in Masai to match some of those the strangers had used.

"A woman in the Council Hall remarked that Masai never wash and don't know what a bath is. I shouldn't have brought them. At least, we shouldn't have gone into a building. Smells aren't quite so bad out of doors. That woman was insulting. I was glad the boys could not understand her there."

"But we do now, some," said Batian. "There was a thing she did not like about us. We do not wear the same clothes, but we are . . . people . . ." He stopped, hesitated, noticing that the pilot was trying so hard not to laugh. "What is it, those words *bath* and *wash?* Something that is a part of water? Is that the meaning? Tell me, please, Bwana. I must know."

As Martin Bolling began to explain, the boys' eyes got rounder and rounder. Use precious water all over one's body when the cattle needed it? Why wasn't grease just as good? It kept the skin from breaking into sores when mosquitoes bit them, and fat was a part of cows, the best animals on earth, Engai's own.

It was difficult for the Bwana to help the boys understand about the unpleasant odor of old fat that other people disliked, but he tried again.

"I know it is the custom of your people," he said, "but you are the only ones who feel so strongly about cattle as you do, that they are more to be considered than any other animal. It is only natural that other folks in East Africa have their special way of living, too. They have their own customs and habits, and very few use fat except to cook with."

Even then Bolling Bwana was not sure that he had made the boys understand wholly, though they nodded when he asked if they did.

Only Batian spoke out. "But we are the Masai. Everything we do is better than what others do. We are an old people. All this land"—he waved his spear about—"was ours in the beginning. This place Nairobi is where our long ago old men fought other tribes and took their cattle. You did not know that perhaps? But this *bath* and *wash* I must know more about. I have learned a new thing this day, to tell my mother."

The pilot changed direction when they were once more in the air. The great mountain was now at their back, and they were headed toward Tanzania, the country south of Kenya.

Farther on, Bolling Bwana waved a hand at them, showing the direction they should look, and the plane came down lower so that they could see some bomas here and there, the little huts hugging the land as their own did. But near each of them lay a field. Women were working in the dried-up ground, pulling up dead weeds and breaking the clods with their hands. It would be seedtime when there was water. The boys looked at each other and shook their heads. Those glances said that they were a little ashamed. Only Masai lived in bomas, but their women didn't plant fields. What did it mean?

The bomas seemed to be coming closer. Ah, the plane was slowly descending. The pilot set them down near a pleasant clump of trees.

The Bwana said he was hungry. Perhaps they were, too? He had brought milk for them and some fruit. It was a kind he was sure they would like because a Masai medicine man of long ago had prescribed *banana* as a fine dry-weather food.

The milk was colder than they were accustomed to because it was in a European bottle called a *Thermos* instead of a gourd. The coldness had to be explained, and the way to eat the yellow-skinned fruit, before they found out why the Bwana had chosen this place to eat in. He wanted them to know about those bomas and fields.

"A change of ways has come to some Masai," he said, "though your people are refusing it. These bomas

Sky Ride

belong to Masai moranes who can never go back to their tribe again because they have married girls from the Warusha people. They speak Masai, so they probably came from the same ancient stock as your tribe did. The Warusha women are taught how to grow food, so they have been making fields out of land that their lawmakers said must be left free for wild animals to graze upon. But there was need of more food for people to eat, too. Here in Tanzania they will have to decide what is best to do for all. Do you understand why I have brought you here? No? Then I must say it in the best way I know. The Masai people, no matter where they live, in Kenya or Tanzania, must learn that they may not have their own way if it hurts other people. No one tribe may. If change is right, it must come. The Masai must learn this."

The boys only looked at him. Even Batian had nothing to say. The milk and bananas had disappeared.

The Bwana rose. "Come," he said. "One more sight and then we will go back to your boma, or your mothers will be sure I have stolen you. I am going to show you that school I spoke of to Ole Likimani yesterday. He has never seen it, but I can tell you that it is a very pleasant place, the Green Valley School. A few of the lawmakers at Nairobi are Masai. Ah, you didn't know that? It was in a school like this one we shall see that they learned about laws and why we must have them and how to make them for the good of the most people at one time. Perhaps one of you will . . . someday. No? That, too, we shall see. Come!"

The three boys were shaking their heads.

"We are to be moranes and hunt lions," said Batian proudly. "That is what a Masai boy must do. You didn't know, Bwana?"

Martin Bolling laughed. "Let us go and look at the school anyway. A short flight and we shall be there. Then you can say you have seen it, near that big Engorongoro Crater, place of a burned-out volcano, where there are thousands of wild animals. They do not hurt the school, and the school does not hurt them. The children aren't there now, not in this 'last month of hunger,' but they will return when the 'month of clouds' begins. Come!"

Batian walked very slowly to the plane. He was thinking.

Why had this journey been made? First to Nairobi town where the people had been so rude. Then to see some women who were married to Masai moranes, breaking the law of Tanzania. And now to look at a school where Masai children were taught the way of Europeans. Did they waste a great deal of water to clean their bodies at that school? *Wash* and *bath*. Ugh! He could not imagine living in that way.

He clutched his spear more tightly as he climbed into the plane, and he did not show any interest when they flew low over the school buildings. They were not as high or as large as those they had seen in Nairobi, but they weren't bomas either. He was glad when he sensed that the pilot was turning and that they were going back to the little plateau they had found so recently, where they would build a new boma and take care of their cattle. Had the little calf missed him today? Had his mother remembered to feed her?

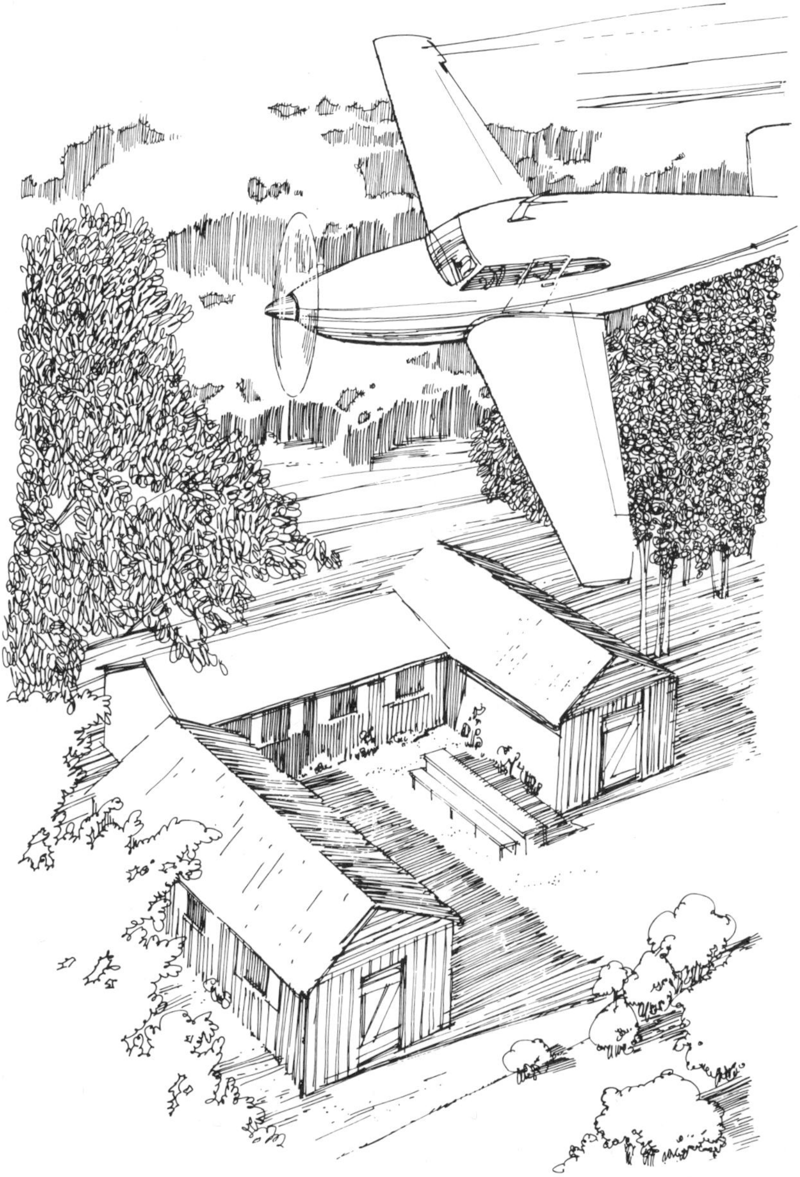

All three of the Bwana's passengers fell asleep on the way back to the boma.

When the pilot noticed how still they were, heads against each other's shoulders, he grinned at the District Officer, who nodded. Into the intercom he said, "I'm afraid you haven't accomplished much today."

"Give them a year or two," said the Bwana. "All the Masai will have some rough experiences in the time just ahead unless they are willing to change some of their ways, or change them whether willing or not. For their own pride, before the whole world, the wild animals must be protected by the Kenya and Tanzania governments. Yet we have to recognize that the Masai were here first, as they claim, so they have some natural rights. But they can get along without quite so many cows if they'd only admit it. They'll have to learn the trick. If they could be made to see that by raising better stock in future and not scorning money the way they do, they could sell some of their extras! But we've got a lot of work ahead of us to convince their medicine men and their Elders that compromise must come if they hope to survive."

"Indeed you have," said the pilot, and then he turned and looked behind him for a long moment at the handsome young faces, so proud and stubborn, even in sleep.

7

Looking Backward and Looking Forward

When the boma came in sight, the Bwana prepared to awaken the boys. It would never do that they should appear to have been indifferent to their ride in the sky. The people of the tribe would not understand that they might be tired by excitement and possibly a little worried about all they had seen. It hadn't been an ordinary experience for them.

That would be especially true for the one named Batian, the officer thought. That boy had asked more questions, and good ones, than either of the other two. If any of the children of his boma should be sent to a school outside, Batian would be the best choice. He'd learn faster than many.

It was too bad that his tribe was still so firmly bound to their old ways. Surprisingly enough, Ole Likimani wasn't. He was shrewd as well as wise. He had been pleased when he heard of the extent of today's planned trip and had allowed the officer to see that he approved of sending some of the children to school, though not any girls. But the men of the boma did not see the advantage to all that school learning for a few would bring.

The Bwana sighed and touched the sleeping boys gently.

The pilot was setting them down very slowly to avoid trouble, because many of the people of the boma could be seen running wildly out to meet them. There were others, standing still, as if they had been rooted in the same spot for the full two hours of the flight.

Batian released Soko's clinging hand before they stepped out of the plane. "Don't let them see you were afraid," he cautioned.

"Weren't you, too?" Soko asked.

"Some," Batian whispered. "We'll talk about it later, when we are once more herding. Yes?"

Soko nodded. "I'd like to do it again," he said, sounding very brave now that they were safely returned to the boma.

The people were acting as if the boys had been away for many days instead of two hours, it seemed to Batian. Soko's father leaned down and touched the boy's head in the Masai way of greeting. And there was Ole Kantai waiting to do the same for him.

Siamanta stood watching, behind his father. She had given the baby boy back to his mother, but she still held the little heifer by the bell thong as if she hadn't let it out of her sight in all the time he had been away. Her eyes still shone with her pride and interest of the morning, when she had urged him to run so as to be

Looking Backward and Looking Forward 89

first at the plane. That look of hers now made Batian feel a little taller somehow.

He looked around. Nothing here was changed, the people, the new boma, the cattle out on the grassland at their sparser and sparser grazing, nothing.

Siamanta said, "Your thoughts are quiet ones, my herdboy. See, the little calf does know you. Couldn't you touch her head, give her a true Masai greeting?"

The calf moved closer and butted his knees.

Batian took the bell thong in his free hand after he had touched the heifer's head, and his mother said, "Come, I have food for you."

He wasn't hungry, but it might be her way to make a chance to ask him questions and so be the first to hear his story. That way she would have most, she probably thought, to tell to the other women while they were building the new manyatta for the boma's five soon-to-be moranes. Each age-set must have its own house.

Before Batian could speak, refuse food, or accept it, there was a great shout from the crowd still standing around the plane, and the two turned to see Ole Kantai stepping up and in.

"What is going to happen? What are they doing?" said Batian.

They watched while two other men followed his father. The door closed, and the plane took off. Were there going to be rides to Nairobi all day? Would the men come back with more to tell than the boys had?

No, the pilot was only circling above and coming down again. Even that brief sight of the boma and its surroundings from a height would be an addition to the riders' daily conversation for a long time to come.

Batian decided that he was hungry, after all. Now was the time for him to talk with his mother, while he could.

But he did not tell her all that he might have. When it came to *bath* and *wash,* he omitted that part. She wouldn't understand, and it might make her sad that he had learned of such things when she had been so anxious for him to be chosen to make that strange journey.

Yes, Nairobi was a big place. No, the people didn't live in bomas. Their buildings were almost as high as the sky. And there were roads for their jeeps, and special places made alongside where the people walked. Some talked and some listened in the great hall where laws were being made.

He tried to describe the Council Hall and laws, but Siamanta only nodded vaguely and was more interested when he told about the school.

No, it was closed, so he didn't see what the children did. Yes, it seemed a nice place. The buildings were different from a manyatta. No, the Bwana had not said what the boys and girls ate at that school.

When their talk was over, Batian realized that he hadn't told her about those other women who had fields beside their bomas. It would probably be so surprising that she would think about it a great deal and ask more questions than he was able to answer. Those men must have liked the Warusha women very much to marry with them and give up belonging to their own people forever.

It took a long time for the village to settle down during that late afternoon and evening after the Bwana had finally flown away with his pilot to Nairobi town.

Batian went to his pallet early. He hadn't done any herding all day, but he was tired from the much talking and laughter in the boma about the boys' journey.

It was unpleasantly warm in the hut, but he knew it was cool outside. There seemed to be more flies tonight, too. The Masai always had them, but as the rainy season approached, the number increased. Batian brushed a few away futilely, for they came back, or others took their place. The people in Nairobi didn't seem to be bothered by flies, now that he thought of it. In spite of his interest in those two new words he had learned in Nairobi, *bath* and *wash,* he didn't associate the flies in the boma with the odor of blood that constantly hung about or with the greasy bodies of the people.

He pulled the little calf closer for comfort, though her soft body was so warm against him. He would be glad when she was strong enough to go with him to the herding. He could look after her all day long then, and he could do it well. Next month would be November, the "time of clouds," and everything would be better. The rain would come and new grass, and the children who went to the Green Valley School would be returning there. The Bwana said they learned many things for five days at a time, and then they went to their bomas for two days. The *Waingereza*—the English— had a name for that, too. *Weekend.* He hadn't told his mother about that, either. He didn't know why he had not. He himself would like to forget that part of today's journey. What had he to do with school when he was going to be a morane, like those whose ceremony was about to be held, and own many calves like this one here by his side?

Gradually the people outside stopped the laughter and talk and went away to their own huts. Batian's father and mother came in, but did not speak to him after they settled on their buffalo skins. Still Batian did not sleep. Through the air vents in the hut, the night sounds of the bush and plain could be heard, giving him more to think about. The high-pitched cry of a prowling hyena made him clutch the little calf even closer to him. Twice he had seen a lion seize a calf and drag it away to tear apart and the hyenas gather around to wait until he was through with his meal so that they could strip the bones that were left.

Closer there came a whistling sound. A lively little breeze had swept across a thorn tree. He knew what it was and wasn't at first afraid. And then fear came. Some of the women must have gathered bunches of a whistling thorn tree and woven them into a nearby part of the fence around the boma. It hadn't been noticed before, but now in the quiet of the night, some animal must have tried to get in and caused the whistling. That was a better explanation than a wind. Little ants bored their way into a long, thick thorn and raised a colony inside it, with food for the taking around them, and when their short lives had ended, the entrance hole was left, making a kind of pipe that made a musical sound when a wind passed over the tree or it was shaken some other way.

Batian stiffened in his place and lay that way a long time before he was satisfied that the prowling wild one had gone away. The sound did not come again, and he relaxed and finally fell asleep with one hand clutching firmly the bell thong around the heifer's neck.

Two days later the women began gathering together the thorn and sapling materials for the new manyatta. It was a long structure like several huts thrown together with some separate rooms inside and no protecting fence without.

Soko, whom Batian met down on the plain each morning, was still full of wonder about all the things they had seen when they flew with the Bwana. He talked boastfully of what he'd like to do the next time. Surely the Bwana, that kind man, would take them on some other day?

"But you shut your eyes part of the time," Batian accused. "How could you have seen all you say?"

Soko said, "I heard much, you cannot deny. My family does not know I didn't see what I told them. They have no thought that I was afraid. I've had great praise. You'll not tell and spoil it?"

Batian grinned. "No, I won't tell," he promised. "But I'm not sure that I want to go again, ever, and I really saw. I want to stay here and someday raise many cattle."

"But the Bwana says we must not have so many. We must raise fewer and better animals. That will be best for all," Soko argued.

So his companion had really listened, at least some of the time, Batian thought. He was speaking true.

"But I mean to have fine ones," Batian said, voicing that ambition for the first time. Not even to his mother had he spoken thus.

"It will be as it will be," Soko countered. "The Laibon will read the stars and tell us what is going to happen, no matter what those men in the Council Hall at

Nairobi rule. This land is ours, and we are never to forget that, so my father says."

Batian nodded. Soko's father was only one among many others, but it was well known in the tribe how most felt about Kenya's laws and change.

He himself wished that Soko would stop talking about their journey to Nairobi. Though he didn't want to, he kept thinking about that Green Valley School, wondering what it was like and how the children could live the different life there for five days and come back to their bomas for two and be comfortable anywhere. How would the *bath* and *wash* be managed at each change? The Bwana had not explained that.

8

A Gift for Batian

The building of the manyatta went on steadily under a pale blue sky. It would be a lovely deeper blue when the weather became colder. Now the sun was burning the color away. The days were long and hot and the cows more and more difficult to look after. They were so hungry that they strayed, and there was danger if they got too far away from the herd. Lions were hungry, too, and therefore more watchful.

Without meaning it, Batian's thoughts constantly went back over the moments he had liked best during the trip with the Bwana. He didn't want to admit even to himself that because of that short two hours his herding time now seemed very long and unexciting. He had been contented before, but not since.

He must be careful not to let Soko guess.

That was why he welcomed Guhano all the more when his friend began to move his herd closer to Batian's. Because Guhano hadn't run quite fast enough, he had not been chosen to go to Nairobi, so all their talk had to be about boma happenings. Guhano didn't ask questions about the other two boys' strange experience.

There had been several new babies born recently, and the women who weren't working on the manyatta had had the usual feasts and celebrations to honor the mothers and their little boys and girls. It was only when the time came to give the newborn their names that the fathers had a part.

One of the births had been in Guhano's own household—his father had three wives—and he had brought Batian a piece of the ox meat that had been roasted there, to eat at midday.

"They did the same for us when we were born," said Guhano as they chewed, "but I don't remember it."

"No one does," said Batian. "What is the first thing you do remember when you were small?"

Guhano thought hard for a moment before he said, "I think it was when we were moving to a new boma and I was sitting on top of the load on my mother's donkey, and I fell off. Instead of comforting me when I cried, she spanked me for that. She said I was a Masai, and they never showed their feelings when anything hurt them. I know now that that is true."

"Have you ever cried since then?" Batian asked.

"Never," said Guhano.

The boy's lips were pressed together in a tight line, and Batian knew that there must have been times when his friend would have liked very much to cry and let his feelings show, and also that he hadn't. Guhano was a truthful one. That, too, was a Masai custom.

A Gift for Batian

"What is your first remembering?" Guhano asked.

"I think it was the time I was told I had been named for one of our long ago chiefs. I didn't like being called Batian because it didn't sound like the names of other boys I played with. It isn't like yours at all."

Guhano grinned. "How do you feel about it now?"

Batian shrugged and then asked, "You won't make fun if I tell?"

"No."

"I have changed my mind. I like it now because it is different."

"But if you liked, you could exchange names with your father. He did. That's why he has Ole before his name. But if you don't want to . . ."

"No, I don't," said Batian precisely.

Guhano stood up then to run after a straying cow. He pointed at her. "There's one that likes being different. She will not stay with the herd. But you . . ." He looked Batian up and down for a moment before he added, "You will be a good Masai in all things."

He ran off to urge the wayward cow to come back where she belonged, and the boys were not close together the rest of the morning. But Batian was to remember what Guhano had said a good many times in the coming days.

It was rumored in the boma that as soon as the manyatta was finished, the Laibon meant to study the stars again and name the day for the five new moranes' ceremony.

But before that could happen, Batian had a surprise that quite put out of his head all his recent impressions of Nairobi, which had filled his thoughts during the long days with the herd.

One morning his father stopped him when he was starting out to help his mother pick the ticks off their cattle. The man and the boy were alone in the hut. Siamanta was already at work.

Ole Kantai sat by the fire hole, though there were no coals in it at this early moment of a hot day to come. He was drinking blood from his gourd cup.

He said, "Wait, boy. The time has come for some words to be spoken."

Ole Kantai's serious tone was unusual enough for Batian to be alarmed. His heart leaped and then steadied to a little faster beat. Had he been faulty in his herding? Was his father displeased about that, or was it something else that had gone wrong? What could it be?

But it did not seem to be anything bad, rather the opposite, when Ole Kantai spoke again.

"It is known in the boma that the Bwana was pleased with you when you rode with him to Nairobi town. That is good."

He drank again, looking at Batian over the rim of his cup.

"You are my oldest son."

"Yes, my father," said Batian, still wondering what was coming. He thought of the baby boy in the hut on the left side of their gateway and was glad that he had come first to be that oldest son.

"Someday you will have many cattle," Ole Kantai went on.

"I will," the boy thought, "if those men in that Council Hall in Nairobi don't change things so that the Masai will have fewer when I am through with being a morane."

A Gift for Batian

Aloud, Batian said, "It is the hope of every morane," speaking very formally.

Ole Kantai nodded and set down the empty gourd. "I have seen how you care for the young heifer, and I think it is not too soon for your own herd to begin, though they may not think so in the boma. But they do not know my oldest son as I do."

He rose and reached for the bell leather on the little heifer's neck and drew her between them. Then he took Batian's hand and guided it through the thong, beneath his. "So . . . I give you this one, out of my herd, to be the beginning of yours from this day. May she be the mother of many in the time to come, before you, as a grown morane, take a wife who will build your first hut for a new family."

Releasing Batian's hand, he leaned over and placed his on the boy's head. It was more than the Masai people's formal greeting in that moment.

Batian felt awed. A heifer of his own! Especially

this one that he had tended according to Masai custom since the little thing had been born. He had fed her, and she had warmed him on cold nights, and he had carried her on the march to this new boma so that she would not be trampled. He had done that for his father. Now she was his. None of the other boys he knew had been so considered by their fathers.

What had the Bwana said about that trip to Nairobi? To whom? Only Ole Likimani would have known. There was nothing he himself had done that was different unless the Bwana might have noticed that Soko was afraid and had not suspected that he, Batian, was . . . well, a little bit, too.

He led the heifer to her resting place, a little platform built against the wall of the hut, where Siamanta would look in on her and see that she was safe and comfortable and out of the sun. In only a few days more she would be able to go out with him when he herded the cattle, and he would tend her there and guard her from the dangers of the bush.

It was another day he would never forget, he thought, as later that morning he talked to the cattle or stood dreamily watching them, leaning against his sturdy small spear.

He wondered if all the calves his father seemed to think she would someday bear would be as beautiful as their mother? And as gentle. Well, no, they wouldn't be that if they were strong, vigorous bull calves. But all those future animals would have to be seen to be known. He could wait. He had years yet to become a morane, but by that time he could be the owner of quite a respectable herd if the laws allowed.

A Gift for Batian

What about the sheep and goats that a Masai usually owned, as well as cattle? Might he trade the first calf to come for a pair of kids? He'd like them to be smooth, sleek black ones, like the nanny and her one little fellow that his father had chosen as part payment for Tipis's spear.

It took his breath away to have such thoughts for the future. He tried to count on his fingers the number that would multiply in a short time, but gave it up impatiently. Did those boys who went to the Masai school learn counting so that they could have told him the answer at once? In that one way, going to school might be a good thing.

How had it come about that today was the one when he had received such a special gift? Had his father consulted the Laibon and found that it was written in the stars as an auspicious one for making gifts? If he had, then surely he, Batian, Masai herdboy, could be sure that he would one day own many fine cattle.

He went to sleep that night with his hand on the calf's soft neck and did not notice that the number of flies buzzing about was worse than ever.

9

The Whistling Thorn

The new manyatta, a scant mile away from the boma, was finished, firm and dry inside and out. The merciless sun, so hard on the people and the animals, had served the women's purpose well. Now the ceremony for the young moranes could be held whenever the Laibon consulted the stars and found an auspicious day, so that Ole Likimani could give the word. Surely it must happen shortly, for the month of white clouds was coming, and how could the people celebrate in pouring rain?

All five moranes were ready. Their hair had grown long enough to plait into many little braids all over their heads. Their spears and shields were waiting. Let the day come.

While the people waited, the news that one boy, though young, had been given an animal of his own, and a heifer at that, gave them something else to talk about. It was not an unheard of thing, the gossipers granted, but for such a smart man, Ole Kantai had surely blundered. That was the opinion of many. Why hadn't he given Batian a bull calf so that it might bear the boy's name, as was their custom, and the two could grow up together, one in everything? There was no better way to teach a Masai child how he should regard all cattle—not alone his father's—with great affection.

There were others who stood by Ole Kantai's choice. Had not the boy Batian shown himself in a short time to be a good herdboy? Already he had a regard for all the animals. Look at the way he had carried that calf on their tedious journey to this new boma. And had not the Bwana spoken well of him after the flight to Nairobi? Must they criticize everything Ole Kantai did? Were they jealous of his standing in the boma?

The argument, only suspected by Ole Kantai because of chance bits he overheard, went on and on and was only stopped when, at evening several days later, Ole Likimani gave the expected report. Tomorrow had been found by the Laibon to be the very best day possible to usher the five young men of the boma into their new position.

They held the ceremony at the new manyatta, and everybody went except the few older men who had seen many such rites. They were accustomed to stay behind and look after the animals of all owners when there was a special occasion of any kind.

Each new morane was dressed by his family at home. Neck and shoulders were anointed with fresh grease. The many little plaits of hair were divided into three groups in front and bound at the ends with short tassels. In the back they were woven together intricately to form a brief pigtail. Then the whole was flattened down with a liberal spreading of paste made of cow fat and the red clay of the region.

A new garment, a long piece of red cloth draped across the boy's shoulders but leaving his arms bare, was his ceremonial dress. The stretchers in his earlobes were removed and heavier ones inserted. A band of buffalo horn was slipped onto his left arm high above the elbow, to last his lifetime. A necklace of large colored beads was fastened around his neck.

Above all he wore a crown of ostrich feathers, set securely in a leather band. Later, when the new morane had killed his first lion, if he had not already killed one, he would wear its mane at ceremonial times.

Batian walked all around Tipis admiringly, as one by one the special symbols of his cousin's new position were added.

Next came his weapons, the sword fastened at his right side, and a club thrust through his belt. The long oval shield, to be carried always in the left hand, was made of buffalo hide and painted in white, red, and black designs known to all Masai.

The greatest moment of all came when Tipis's father brought out the great spear seven feet long. Though Batian had seen it before, today it was a fearsome-looking thing, he thought. It was at least two feet taller than Tipis when he let it rest on the ground, holding it in his right hand as he must always do.

The lower end was pointed so that it could be

The Whistling Thorn

pushed into the earth and stand by itself when that might be necessary. The wood of the shaft was shining with grease. At the top the wide, sharp-pointed metal blade took up fully two and a half feet of the whole length. It made the spear a deadly weapon.

Batian shivered, partly from the excitement of the morning and partly from imagining what that tip would do to a rushing lion in combat. His own spear looked shrunken somehow and like a toy, measured against a man's weapon. It had never seemed so before.

At the last, Tipis's mother brought a small bunch of grass, the Masai symbol of peace, which she fastened firmly in the shoulder knot of his robe. Tipis was then ready for the ceremony, already looking a proud warrior. But he had been turned into a stranger by the splendor of his dress and ornaments and weapons.

The whole family walked with him to the manyatta.

Ole Likimani welcomed the boys as a new age-set, all being fifteen together, within the boma. Now that they were become warriors, he said, though the Bwana's people in Nairobi had forbidden Masai tribes to fight among each other as they had in ancient times, they must conduct themselves fully as mightily as those old ones had done when any occasion arose.

"It begins to seem," he added, "that perhaps hereafter we must fight with our minds for our lands and rights, if that, too, comes."

Then the new warriors danced for the people, trying to show in mimic style what a lion hunt was like. First they stalked for a victim, then having pretended to find one, they made wild thrusts with the great spears, uttering deafening yells. They leaped high in the air. Their faces wore fierce expressions as they rushed forward, the great shields held close to their bodies, to kill the springing lion. Some of their newly plastered hair came lose and flapped about with every move. It was so real that the smallest children were frightened, and their cries added a shriller note to the noise.

When the sham fight was over, the five new warriors sat down on the dirt floor of the manyatta, as if there was no more battle in them, though everybody knew they were only breathless from the exercise. They were allowed to rest a little, and then it was time for the ceremonial feast.

Two fathers of the five had given oxen, and there was a wonderful smell of roasting meat when the people came out of the manyatta after the dancing was over.

Batian and Soko and Guhano stood at one side, watching the preparation for serving.

"Someday we will be doing this," said Guhano. "We are the same age-set. We will raise our families in the same boma, and one other day . . ." He hesitated.

"Yes, go on," said Batian.

"I don't like to think of it . . . the time when we shall be old men together."

Soko said, "Then don't think of it. There will be many cows between us and that time. And there will be stories to tell, such stories that all in the boma will listen and think us very great men."

"We must first become warriors, as have these this day," Batian reminded them.

Soko nodded. "Does it hurt very much, the first part

The Whistling Thorn

of becoming a warrior? That which they call circumcision?"

Guhano looked doubtful. "No one has ever said. They do not speak of it. So we shall not. Come, they are calling us to get our pieces of meat."

Toward the end of that month called "last of hunger," before the rain clouds could be expected, Batian could not wait any longer when the chance was given him to take the heifer to pasture. He had named her by that time—Nyenpe, the Masai word for "pale." It described her perfectly, white face and light brown coat, and she was learning to answer to it.

The days after the moranes' ceremony had been very dull for all the herdboys, especially for Soko and Batian, who had the flight to Nairobi to add to the contrast of long days when nothing happened, not even a birth, to occasion a feast in the boma. The heat was bad enough and so was the growing hunger of the cattle. They were thinner-seeming every day. The boys needed help to manage them, and the old men began to come out to the plain regularly, though they grumbled.

Siamanta hadn't said anything that showed her interest in the increasing strength of the calf until one morning when she surprised Batian by handing him a small gourd full of milk as he was about ready to set off with the herd.

"You will need this for Nyenpe today perhaps if you plan to take her with you?" she said, artfully leaving the decision to him. "Your father thinks she is big enough now."

Batian's eyes shone. "Now? Today? It will be all right?"

Siamanta nodded and mimicked him. "Now. Today. All right, as your father says. She followed you to the door yesterday morning, and you did not see. She is getting tired of this place and of me. I am only another female."

The boy grinned at her and reached for the gourd. He walked proudly out of his family's gateway a few minutes later, with Nyenpe held close beside him by her bell thong. This time, he was remembering, she did not need to be carried, and he had food for her. That other time he hadn't thought of it. He would tend her faithfully this day, and she would return with him at night to sleep beside him still, safe from harm. She was his now, for all the days they'd be together. It was a right thing his father had done, making such a gift, no matter what was thought in the boma. They would see.

There were three full days of peaceful routine out on the plain with the herds before the thing happened that changed a great deal of boma thinking.

That fourth morning was sultry. It was hard to breathe, and everyone knew that the time of the white clouds was coming fast. The cows were restless and seemed uneasy, raising their heads and bawling occasionally. The birds were quiet, and the boys and men with the herds were not aware of the usual sounds that told them there were peaceable wild animals about, though they couldn't see them.

Batian and Guhano had drawn their cattle in closer to the thickets that marked the beginning of the bush.

The Whistling Thorn

There was a little protection for them from the midday sun, so they risked the constant fear that a lion or a leopard would raid.

When, about noontime, Nyenpe butted Batian's knee, he knew that she was hungry, and he had unslung the gourd, hung over his shoulder by a strap, when he heard a familiar sound behind him. Something had brushed against a clump of whistling thorn in the thicket. It had to be an animal because there hadn't been the slightest movement of air all morning, not even a momentary little dust whirl that might be expected at this time of year. It could be the awaited lion or leopard after the cattle.

The sound came again.

Batian whirled and saw, half hidden by drying leaves, the head of a half-grown lion. He could tell by the set of its shoulders that it was preparing to spring. The eyes were deep yellow in the sunlight, gleaming with cruel anticipation of the wonderful meal that the tender young body of Nyenpe would make for him.

Anger surged through Batian's whole body like a flaming wave. It would be a life-long disgrace for him to let that beast get one of the herd and Nyenpe most of all.

He yelled for Guhano, dropped the gourd, and thrust the calf behind him. Then he threw his spear with all his strength just as the beast sprang. He had been so shaken that he hadn't aimed. There wasn't time, besides.

As the beast shot past him and he smelled its strong odor, he felt a great blow on his shoulder. As he fell,

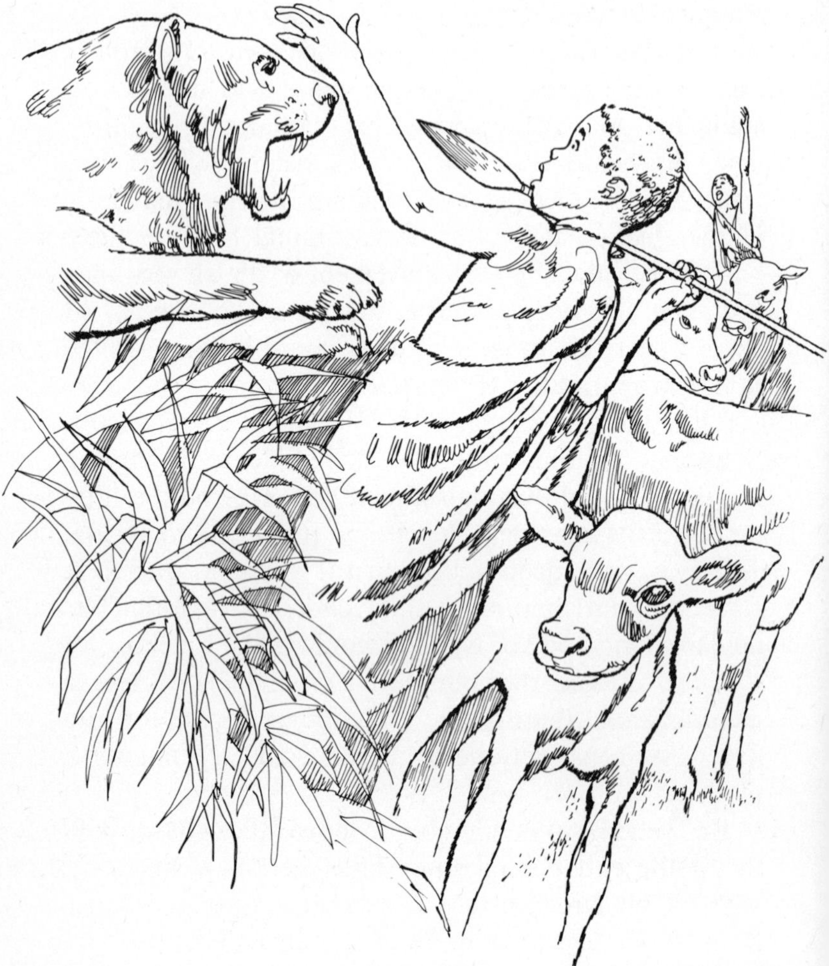

The Whistling Thorn

he heard Guhano shouting and realized that the cattle were stampeding. "Someone should stop them," he thought faintly, "or they'd be . . ."

When he roused, he was still lying on the ground, but he saw that Guhano, kneeling beside him, was all right, and he held Nyenpe securely by her bell thong. She wasn't harmed, either. The Laibon was there, too, and Ole Kantai, and beyond them half the village seemed to have come out.

The Laibon was doing something to his shoulder, moving it about, and it hurt, but he remembered not to cry out. Instead, he asked, "The cattle? Are they . . . safe? Did the lion . . . kill?" By that time he was panting with the shoulder pain.

Ole Kantai said, "It hadn't time, boy. Your spear got in its way. You should see where it is. We haven't taken it out yet, so that you might look for yourself."

Guhano couldn't wait for Batian to get up and look. He said, "Right through the eye! He was dead before he came down. Soko ran for the Laibon and your father, and they sent men after the cattle. We think all are safe. Every man's herd."

Nyenpe pushed past Guhano and began to lick Batian's face. He did not mind the feeling. He was used to that little rough tongue now, and it kept the flies away.

The Laibon stood up. "It is only a deep bruise," he said. "I think the lion's hind foot gave the boy's shoulder a great slap as he passed. It will be very painful for several days, but the skin did not break."

The spilled milk had soaked Batian's robe, and Nyenpe was licking what she could. She ought to have a good feed.

Batian felt dizzy when he sat up, but the Laibon said that that would go away if he waited a moment before he tried walking.

He noticed then, briefly, that the Laibon and his father and several of the other fathers were looking very solemn. They ought to be smiling and full of relief that the lion hadn't done much harm. He wondered about it a little before he started back to the boma, with Soko on one side and Guhano on the other, to get more milk for the calf.

10

A Gourd Full of Cow Fat

It was not long before Batian found out the reason for the strange expressions on his father's and the Laibon's faces.

The whole boma was dismayed because, though so young, he had killed a lion. Nothing like that had ever before happened, not in that tribe. It was a young warrior's best way to prove himself, his courage and bravery. But sometimes a new morane was not able to qualify with a dead lion to his credit until some time after his formal ceremony and beginning life in his age-set manyatta.

Now here was young Batian, son of Ole Kantai, who had only become a herdboy a few months before, proving already his warrior qualities. Or was he? What was to be done about him?

Ole Likimani did not know, and he asked the Laibon and the other two Elders who were in authority with him what they thought.

No one in the whole boma had an answer that all could agree on because opinion was divided about the act itself. Praise was not unanimous. The boy had let the cattle drift too close to the thorn thicket, where there was perfect hiding for a lurking lion.

Others said it wasn't skill or bravery. The spear had gone through the lion's eye by pure chance. The boy was fortunate to have escaped with his own life, let alone the safety of his calf. It was all right to feel the way he did about the heifer. That was a good sign that he would be alert to protect his herd when he had grown up and owned one.

But now? Why make the occasion seem so important? Couldn't he go on in the usual way of a herdboy and let the boma treat the lion business only as an unusual happening, never heard of before and not likely to occur ever again? Couldn't they?

It became quite noticeable, when the arguing grew heated, that those who wanted to make little of Batian's bravery were fathers of sons who were rather slow at learning to herd properly and dull in other ways.

Batian was aware of all the talk. What he himself didn't hear was repeated to him at every opportunity. And there were also the peculiar looks that followed him everywhere, so that he became as anxious as his puzzled elders for an ending. He even began to feel a little bit guilty about the whole thing.

He knew he had been extremely fortunate. But when no one could find anything more to say, he reviewed it for himself as it had actually happened. He had done the only things that seemed sensible that morning. He had herded the cattle close to the thicket for their comfort. He had tried to protect the heifer first, but all the other animals as well, with the one desperate cast of his spear. It was all he had time for. The lion, still young, was not experienced possibly. He himself had not been a herdboy long. If his spear had swerved only a little, the beast could have easily clawed him savagely and killed the calf. He was surprised his arm had been so steady when he was madly angry.

Altogether he disliked thinking as much about it as he had been obliged to. The animal's mane hadn't yet filled out, so he hadn't a trophy to keep for the time when he'd become a morane. But he'd have the memory all his life.

Ole Likimani listened patiently to all the talk and thought about everything that had been said for a few days longer before he sent for the Bwana to help them.

Then the grumblers said that that should have been done in the first place, forgetting that such haste was not the Masai custom.

They all had to wait again for Ole Likimani's plan to be acted upon because the only way to invite Martin Bolling to their boma was to send out a runner. A really good one could do fifty miles in a day. He must then find another one at the next possible boma who would carry the message another fifty miles the next day, and so the word would eventually reach Nairobi town. And if the Bwana was there and not out on safari in another direction, presumably he would start at once in the airplane. He would know where he was to bring it down when he was reminded that he had once taken three boys from that boma on a two-hour flight.

It took three days for Martin Bolling to receive the anxious message, but he came. Ole Likimani had asked the Laibon's oldest son to watch for the plane, and when the young man heard its distant humming sound, he came running in to announce it.

The old man gathered up his scanty rust-red robe, grasped his spear firmly, and summoning the other two Elders, he made for their pleasant knoll under the shade trees to wait for his guest.

The village followed, as many as were free just then to do so, but they stood at a respectful distance. They could not speak at such a meeting unless invited, but they would be present if needed.

Batian was out with the cattle and Nyenpe with him, but he heard all the details of that gathering later, the part that took place before he was summoned.

Bolling Bwana looked very grave when Ole Likimani finished the story about the lion. At the end of it, he summed up their worry in one sentence.

He said, "Batian is too young to become a morane now by all the customs of the Masai, observed through many generations," and added in a trembling voice, "Tell us what to do, Bwana."

The village would have been shocked if they could have read their District Officer's mind at that moment. He stood before them with his hands thrust into the pockets of his bush jacket and seemed to be considering his answer. He was thinking, "Blessings on that lion. Now, perhaps they will listen to me and agree with my plan, and thereby help themselves."

Aloud he asked a question, looking directly at Ole Likimani.

"Have you talked with those parents I named, to speak of that business I mentioned when I was last here? That time when I took the three boys to Nairobi town and round and about?"

Ole Likimani, to the surprise of the onlookers, acted as if he felt guilty and shifted his glance.

"I hadn't any hope it would succeed," he said, "but I talked to one father. His wife would have no choice in the decision. They do not vote among us. You know that, Bwana. And the father clings to our old ways, and, as he thinks, so do many. He is powerful in our boma. In opposition to your idea, he gave his son a calf gift the next day, as a beginning for his own herd. I think it was planned to keep the boy even closer to our tribal ways."

"Perhaps now he will see the question somewhat differently?" said Martin Bolling.

Ole Likimani smiled then. "I hope so," he agreed.

It was beyond the Bwana's powers, he thought, to have arranged for a young, hungry lion to be in a particular place at the right time to bring about plans of his own. But there was Engai to whom the Masai had prayed for long years. Was He thinking that it would be good for the future of this tribe to send one of its sons to that crater school?

The listeners were looking at each other wonderingly. Ole Likimani and the Bwana had been using Masai words, as all had heard, but what did they mean? What thing were he and the Bwana talking about? There was only one to be decided today, wasn't there? And that was what to do about young Batian, son of Ole Kantai, who had killed a lion. All knew that it was Ole Kantai who had made the calf gift recently, but that had nothing to do with the lion business. Somehow the Bwana's talk hadn't sounded that way.

That was when they were further surprised because Bolling Bwana asked that young Batian be sent for, to come here to the tree, and his parents with him.

Ole Kantai was already there. He stepped forward, looked around, and motioned to Siamanta from the back row where she stood with the other women. She was timid and had to be persuaded. When had a boy's mother ever been considered in any question about him?

There was a little more delay while arrangement was made for the family herd to be attended in Batian's place, and then the boy came, leading Nyenpe.

By now practically all work in the boma had stopped, as others came hurrying to join the earlier listeners. The word had spread that something exciting had been added to the question about what to do with that boy Batian.

The Bwana was speaking again when they got there. He said, "Batian killed a lion the other day. It was a brave act. And just as that lion was so young that he hadn't yet grown his mane, so Batian is not yet old enough to become a morane, though he has proved that he has the right kind of courage. Someday he will be a worthy warrior, and all the tribe will be proud of him. Before that time comes, there is a special job that Batian can do for all of you."

A little murmur swept over the crowd and was swiftly stilled when the Bwana held up his hand. He looked for a quiet minute at Ole Kantai and at Siamanta, both standing so still before him with their young son between them and the pretty little heifer in front. Then he spoke to them directly, but he lifted his voice a little, and all there heard him distinctly.

"If you thought that Batian could do something very good for the tribe in the next few years, would you be willing for him to do it? Will you allow him to attend the Green Valley School, where there are Masai children from other tribes? He will learn many things about laws and possession of property. He will understand how to help Ole Likimani and the other Elders and the Laibon when they try with words in Nairobi to maintain your land and cattle rights. He will learn also the value of the health of your herds. He will have time for that and to become a morane, too, later if it seems best. Do you understand that to do this he must leave the boma for a while? Someone else will have to look

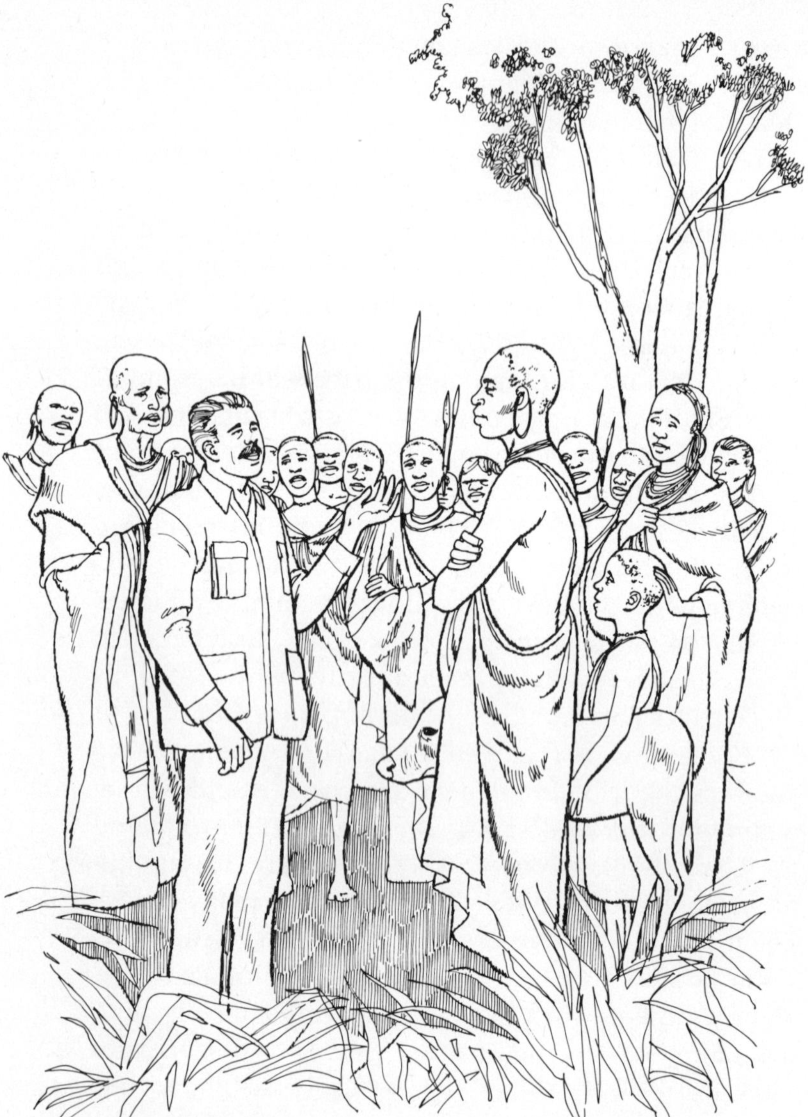

after your cattle while he is away, it is true, but he will be learning to help this whole tribe. Are you willing?"

Siamanta's eyes filled with tears.

Batian clutched Nyenpe's bell thong more tightly.

It was a hard moment for Ole Kantai. He did not notice what his family did. He stared straight ahead, his neck stiff, his right hand clenched on his upright spear. He stood that way for several minutes while the Bwana waited.

Then he heard some of his neighbors behind him, urging softly, "It is the best way, Ole Kantai. Send him to that place. But not alone. Let another boy go with him, so that he will like it better. Speak, Ole Kantai."

The soft whispers grew louder.

The Bwana still waited quietly.

Ole Kantai looked down at his son. "What shall I say?" he asked.

Batian whispered, "Nyenpe?"

Martin Bolling's eyes were kind, though he had to say, "I don't think they let the children take pets to the Green Valley School."

Siamanta said, feeling shameless to be speaking before everybody when assembled together, though it was directly to her son, "I will raise her for you, my herd-boy, and she will have the best care that any cow has ever had in any boma where I have built."

Batian looked up at the District Officer then and said, "Soko *and* Guhano, too," firmly, bargaining.

He did not see the look that passed between the Bwana and Ole Likimani, but Ole Kantai did, yet he did not feel defeated, he who had clung to the old ways so long. Somehow, because he would be the first man of his tribe to agree to send his son to a school for the future benefit of all in the boma, he'd be gaining more power, not losing any. And Batian would benefit, too. He would build that promised herd for the boy, more carefully than any other line of cows he had ever owned.

There was argument in Batian's bargaining words, a willingness to go to the Green Valley School if he could have his two friends with him. But he wouldn't have dared to speak that way if he hadn't felt his parents were willing, too, that he should go.

Everybody concerned looked each at the other when he spoke, and then they nodded together, Ole Likimani, Ole Kantai and Siamanta, and the fathers of Soko and Guhano.

The Bwana was pleased.

"Can the boys be ready in two days more?" he asked. "You have delayed so long now that the month of clouds is here, and school has already begun. I know that, but the boys will not be too late if they fly there with me." His hands came out of the pockets of his jacket, and he turned away from the village crowd, ready to leave them to their preparations. "Two days?" he asked again.

Then the voices of three fathers echoed his as they promised, "Two days, Bwana."

The short time they had left went too fast.

An ox was roasted, given by Soko's father surprisingly, for one more village feast before three of its sons left for a strange adventure. The new moranes were invited, but when they came, found they had to take second place. The people were much more interested, quite unnecessarily the warriors thought, in three little herdboys.

There were many at that feast who still did not quite understand what had been going on but which now seemed to have provided the solution to the unusual crisis the lion had caused. It would require some long, patient explanation before they would comprehend. They would find, Ole Kantai hoped, that of late Masai life hadn't been entirely tending cattle.

Batian did not feel guilty any more, but it did seem as if he had been walking in a dream ever since the moment he had raised his spear and thrown it at the springing lion. But Nyenpe was real enough, and he did not see how he could bear to leave her in the boma while he went away to that strange place.

But there were those two-day times, called *weekends,* that he hadn't told his family about. If he was allowed to return to the village once in a while, it would help to leave Nyenpe now. But there were those other two words, *bath* and *wash*. He felt he understood them and wished he could tell Siamanta, though he was afraid she would not. She would say, "Water on one's body? Such a waste of it when we always have plenty of cow fat."

There were probably other wonders waiting for him and Soko and Guhano. He thought of Siamanta's blue beads, dropped into the gourd to keep track of the number of days before they should return to the armorers' boma for the new spears, and the lost total, and of his own impatience because he couldn't multiply on his fingers so that he would know how many cows he might one day raise. Just learning counting would be good, down there at that school across the Kenya border.

When they heard the plane on the appointed morning, the whole boma ran outside to see it land and take off.

Siamanta hurried and got herself a place in the front row. One hand was thrust tightly beneath Nyenpe's bell thong, and Batian kept running back from the door of the plane for one more loving pat. The last time when Martin Bolling said, "No more, Batian. We must go," Siamanta brought her other hand out from beneath her draperies, and in it was a gourd, with some dry grass stuffed in the opening, which she pushed hastily at Batian.

Her voice was trembling when she whispered, "Cow fat, my herdboy, to keep your skin smooth. I almost

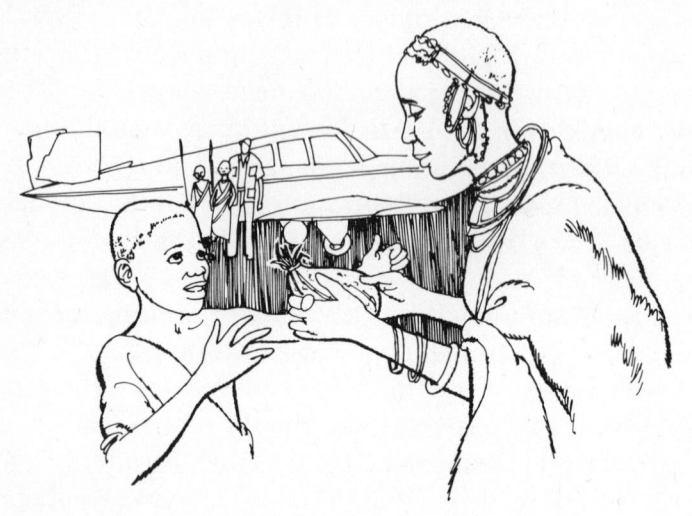

A Gourd Full of Cow Fat

forgot. They won't have any at that place unless they keep cows. But they must get it somewhere, because Bolling Bwana said there would be other Masai children with you."

She laid her hand on his head for a moment, and then he was stepping up into the plane and the door was closing and there was something strange filling his eyes.

He must not let Guhano see, that one who had never cried since the time he was big enough to ride by himself on a donkey load.

Batian sat stiffly in his place for a long time after they were in the air, his spear held tightly in his right hand and the gourd full of cow fat in his left. He couldn't decide whether to be happy or sad that because he, Batian, son of Ole Kantai, had killed his first lion, he was here in Bolling Bwana's plane on his way to a strange new life. If other Masai children could stand it, then he could. He knew now that he had been resisting the idea of going to school, which the Bwana had somehow put in his mind, ever since their other wonderful flight together. He was sure that Soko had not suspected it. But why had he said he would come? What better life could there be than herding cattle, eating roast ox once in a while, and tending little newborn calves? And kids and lambs?

Then he had to lean over and set the gourd carefully on the floor and forget his own sadness because he had felt a small hand clutching his arm.

Soko was afraid again. He'd have to look after him.